CINDERELLA

A Pantomime

by

K. O. SAMUEL

GW00750676

SAMUEL   FRENCH

LONDON

NEW YORK TORONTO SYDNEY HOLLYWOOD

*Printed and Bound in Great Britain by
Butler & Tanner Ltd.,
Frome and London*

CHARACTERS

(in the order of their appearance)

BARON BAMBOOZLE
BARONESS BAMBOOZLE
SPY
COP } (Brokers' Men.)
PRINCE CHARMING
DANDINI
BLUEBELLE
MAYBELLE } (The Ugly Sisters.)
CINDERELLA
BUTTONS
THE WATCHMAN
THE SERGEANT
FAIRY GODMOTHER
THE GUIDE
THE HERALD

Chorus of villagers, huntsmen, guests at the ball, etc.
Fairy ballet.

SYNOPSIS OF SCENES.

1) 4-8 basic pantomime.

CINDERELLA

SCENE 1

Scene.—*The village green.*

The entrance to the Baron's *house is up* r. *and there are the usual side entrances.*

When the Curtain *rises, the stage is filled by the* Chorus *dancing a country dance. As they finish, the* Baron *enters down* r. *As he enters he sings part of the song, " Come into the garden, Maud ". but stops as he reaches* c.

Chorus. Good morning, Baron.
Baron. Good morning, ladies.
Chorus. What a beautiful morning.
Baron. Eh ? I didn't quite catch . . .
Chorus. We said, " What a beautiful morning ".
Baron. My dear girls, I haven't come here to talk about the weather.
Chorus. Oh !
Baron. I've come here to talk about my wife.

(*There is general laughter from the* Chorus.)

(*He regards them reproachfully.*) My wife is not a joke—unfortunately. (*He makes a sudden dive at one of the girls* r. *of him.*) Have you seen the wife pass this way ?
Girl (*drawing back in alarm*). One would think she was the fox.
Baron. The fox ? (*He mutters aside.*) She's the vixen.

(*The* Baroness *enters up* l. *She wears panniers of exaggerated proportions. She moves down* c. *to* l. *of the* Baron.)

Baroness. Oswald !
Baron (*in a servile tone*). Oh, there you are, my darling. I've been looking for you everywhere.

BARONESS.   Oswald, that is just simply *not* true.   *I* have been *everywhere* looking for *you*—so if *you* had been *everywhere*, **we** should have met before—*somewhere*.

(*This is too much for the Baron, and he blinks at her vaguely.*)

BARON.   Haven't we—met before—somewhere ?

BARONESS.   Don't be funny !   I'm your wife—not your stooge. I do wish you would take a *little* interest in the family affairs. You have simply *no* idea of what is going on in your own house, have you ?

BARON.   Well, you are the mistress, my love, and so . . .

BARONESS.   Are you aware that Buttons is missing ?

BARON (*horrified*).   My dear !   Your grammar !

BARONESS.   I repeat—Buttons is missing.   Can you throw any light upon them— (*she corrects herself*) upon *him* ?

BARON.   Oh, Buttons !   I believe he *did* tell me the other day he was going to look for another job.   He had the nerve to ask me for a rise.

BARONESS.   And did you give him a rise ?

BARON (*striving for patience*).   My dear, if I may be allowed to take some of the words out of your mouth—I do wish *you* would take a little interest in our *financial* affairs.   (*He mutters aside.*) Give him a rise.

BARONESS.   What are you going to do about it ?

BARON (*scratching his head*).   I admit that without Buttons it is going to be difficult to keep up—er . . .

BARONESS.   Will you kindly curb your imagination, Oswald, and be practical.   Now that Buttons have gone—(*she corrects herself again*) *has* gone, *I* have no adequate protection.

BARON.   Protection, my love ?

BARONESS.   Are you not aware that two strange men have been hanging about our house all morning—taking notes ?

BARON.   Impossible !   There hasn't been a note in the house for years.

BARONESS.   They are planning to remove the furniture.   *We* must have a plan, too.   A plan of campaign.

BARON.   A can of champagne ?

BARONESS.   You heard what I said.   If *you* don't send those men packing, I shall do it myself.

BARON.   We shall have to do the packing in any case if something doesn't turn up, and, as you never allow *me* to do it, I don't know why I'm dragged into it at all.

BARONESS (*scornfully*). You are *supposed* to be master of the house. I must at least go through the drill.

BARON. You'll go through the window if you interfere with them. (*He points significantly up* R.)

BARONESS. Are they there by your invitation ?

BARON. Not exactly—but they will be there until I can pay what I owe.

BARONESS (*abruptly*). Oh !

BARON. I *said* " owe ".

BARONESS (*pulling herself together and looking around*). Oswald, why are all these people standing round—listening to our private affairs ?

BARON (*amused*). They won't go yet, my dear.

BARONESS. Why not ?

BARON (*to the* CHORUS). Tell her why you won't go yet.

CHORUS. We're waiting to see the Prince.

BARON. They're waiting to see the Prince. He's out hunting to-day. They'll queue up for hours just to get a glimpse of their hero—silly little things. Not sensible people like you and me my dear.

BARONESS (*looking wistful*). I wouldn't mind—seeing the Prince. I shall go in, tidy myself up and join the queue.

BARON (*trying to look jealous*). I'm going green with . . .

BARONESS. You're going *barmy*. Come with me and we'll get rid of those two men.

(*She bustles the* BARON *up* R. *and they exit. The sound of a hunting horn is heard off up* L. *The* CHORUS *cheer.*)

GIRL (*looking off up* L. ; *calling*). There's the Prince.

(*The others form up behind her, and look off. The sound of cheers is heard off.*)

2ND GIRL (*looking off* ; *calling*). There he goes. Come on, girls.

(*The* CHORUS *exit quickly up* L. *There is the sound of commotion off up* R. ; *the noise of furniture being flung about, and angry shouts.* SPY *and* COP *stumble on up* R., *rub their heads and move down* C.)

SPY. I see *you've* had an accident, too.

COP. Something hit me.

SPY. Same here. (*He thinks a moment.*) Nice people in that house.

COP (*coldly*). *Very* nice. Asking us to go, weren't they?

SPY. Something like it. (*A sudden idea strikes him and he faces front, with a gesture.*)

COP. What's the matter?

SPY. It's just struck me.

COP. What—again?

SPY (*looking at* COP). The funny side.

(COP *starts to walk round* SPY.)

What are you doing?

COP. Looking for the funny side.

SPY (*starting to laugh*). I can't help laughing.

COP. What's the joke?

SPY (*trying to stifle his hilarity*). *We're* supposed to be doing the chucking out.

COP (*dolefully*). Now we've got to start all over again.

SPY. Cheer up! Somewhere the sun is shining. Look for the silver lining.

(COP *starts to look inside his clothes.*)

Not there, you fool! (*He points upwards.*) Up there. When you're feeling blue, I'll tell you what to do.

COP. What?

SPY. Sing a song as you jog along.

(COP *moves to the exit down* L.)

Where are you going?

COP. Jogging along—if you're going to sing a song.

SPY. Why don't you join in?

COP (*moving to* L. *of* SPY). Join in?

SPY (*patiently explaining the obvious*). If *you* sing too, you won't be able to hear *me* sing.

COP (*satisfied*). There's something in that.

(SPY *and* COP *sing a topical duet.*)

SPY. Now—let's get down to brass tacks.

COP (*rubbing his posterior*). I've been there already.

SPY. We've got to get inside again, haven't we?

COP. That's it.

SPY. And we don't want to be asked to leave again, do we?

Cop.   Certainly not !

Spy.   Well—have you got any ideas ?

Cop (*brightly*).   We'll put her head in a **bag.**

Spy.   Not so easy.

Cop.   It's as easy as putting a bun in a bag.

Spy.   What sort of a bun d'you think she is ?

Cop.   A hot-cross bun.   (*He goes into fits of laughter at his joke.*)

(Spy *remains serious.*)

Spy (*who is not convinced*).   What will *she* be doing while you're putting her head in a bag ?

Cop.   She won't have time to do anything.   I'll show you. (*He produces a bag.*)   We'll have a run through it.

Spy (*indicating the bag*).   How are you going to run through that ?

Cop.   No, no.   We'll have a *rehearsal*, see ?   *You* engage her in conversation and *I'll* creep up behind and put the bag over her head.   Now, go on—*engage* her.

(Spy *goes into an imaginary tackle.*)

No, no !   Engage her in *conversation.*

Spy.   What do I say ?

Cop.   You say— (*he thinks a moment*) " I'm sorry, madam, if we have caused you any inconvenience, but we are only engaged in the exercise of our daily duties."

(*The rehearsal business can be worked ad lib, after which* Cop *puts the bag over* Spy's *head.*)

That's where I put the bag on, see ?

Spy (*after struggling to get his head out*).   You don't have to put it on *my* head.   (*Annoyed, he smooths his hair.*)   You've spoilt my parting.

Cop.   Come on, let's get cracking.   We'll go round to the back of the house and get in through the scullery window.

Spy.   Wait a minute—supposing the old Baron interferes ?

Cop.   Don't you worry about the Baron.   He won't hurt *us.* When he sees his wife's head in a bag, he'll laugh his own head off.

(Cop *and* Spy *exit down* R.   *The sounds of a hunting horn and cheers are heard off* L.   *The orchestra start the opening bars of* Prince Charming's *entrance number.   Choose a good rousing song.   The* Prince *enters up* L., *with* Huntsmen *in support.   Other members of the* CHORUS *enter and dress the stage. During the song,* DANDINI *enters up* L. *At the end of the song, the* HUNTSMEN *are paired off with the girls of the* CHORUS, *upstage, and the* PRINCE *speaks to* DANDINI *who comes down* C.)

PRINCE. What a welcome! And what a charming village. Upon my soul, Dandini, I don't care if we hunt no more to-day.

DANDINI. Neither would the Hunt—by the look of them.

(*The* PRINCE *and* DANDINI *turn and watch the courting that is now going on between the* HUNTSMEN *and the girls of the* CHORUS.)

PRINCE. I don't blame them. There are other sports than blood sports—eh, Dandini? (*He nudges* DANDINI *and winks.*) When there's quarry like that around, you wouldn't care if you never saw the fox again to-day.

DANDINI (*laughing*). I'm entirely of your opinion, sir.

PRINCE. You're a lucky dog, you know.

DANDINI (*puzzled*). Lucky, sir? Me?

PRINCE. Yes, you.

DANDINI. You mean—lucky to be your companion?

PRINCE. I mean lucky to be free—to hunt where you like. That's what I've never been able to do. Wherever I go, I'm recognized. I can't move anywhere without people running to their house doors and shouting: " There he goes ! "

DANDINI. I wouldn't mind *that*.

PRINCE. You wouldn't?

DANDINI. No, sir.

PRINCE. Then, damme, you shall have a taste of it.

DANDINI. What d'you mean, sir?

PRINCE. I'll tell you. (*Confidentially.*) Get rid of the crowd.

DANDINI (*looking around*). Not so easy.

PRINCE. There's the Hunt breakfast, still untouched. It's a bit late for breakfast, but it's all ready on the Green, yonder. People in love aren't fussy about what time they have breakfast.

DANDINI (*clapping his hands to get the crowd's attention*). Ladies and gentlemen, we hunt no more to-day. You are invited one and all to breakfast—under the spreading chestnut tree.

(*The* CHORUS *and* HUNTSMEN *cheer and exit in groups to music.*)

PRINCE. Here—take my cloak and hat, and give me yours.

(DANDINI *puts on the* PRINCE's *cloak and hat.*)

How d'you feel? D'you think you could take my place?

DANDINI. I'll try, sir—if it will please you.

PRINCE (*laughing*). You rogue—you know you're dying to play the part. And, by gad, I believe you'll do it well. (*He puts on* DANDINI'S *hat.*) Now—watch me bend the knee of servitude. (*He bows, and kisses* DANDINI'S *hand.*) How's that ?

DANDINI. Just as I would do it, sir.

PRINCE. Now *you're* the Prince and *I'm* your servant. (*He slaps* DANDINI *on the back.*) Dandini, we'll get some fun out of this.

(*There is the sound of commotion off up* R. *The voices of the* BARONESS *and* BARON *are heard.*)

(*He moves to the entrance up* R.) There's a row on. Did our fox go to earth there ?

DANDINI (*moving to the* PRINCE). It *does* sound as if we're missing the kill.

PRINCE (*leading* DANDINI *up* C.). Look out, here come the hounds.

(SPY *and* COP *enter up* R. *They have bags over their heads, and their hands are tied behind them. They have eye-slits in the bags but pretend they cannot see where they are going, and bump against each other in their flight. They are followed on by the* BARON *and* BARONESS, *who chase them down* L. *The* BARON *waves a riding-crop.*)

BARONESS (*shouting breathlessly*). Put my head in a bag, would you ? I'll give you hot-cross bun.

(SPY *and* COP *exit hurriedly down* L. *The* BARONESS, *down* L., *becomes aware of the* PRINCE *and* DANDINI.)

(*Aside to the* BARON.) Look, there's the Prince. Do your stuff.

BARON. Stuff ?

BARONESS (*impatiently*). Introduce me, you nit-wit, and be quick or we'll lose our chance.

(*The* BARON *approaches the* PRINCE *and bows.*)

BARON. Your Highness . . .

PRINCE (*aside to* DANDINI). Go on, do your stuff. (*He gives* DANDINI *a nudge.*)

(DANDINI *takes his place.*)

BARON (*puzzled at the shuffle round*). The Prince, I presume ?

DANDINI.   You do.

BARON (*bowing again*).   Your Highness—my wife humbly desires to be introduced.   She is a remarkable woman, sir—noted for her puddings.   You've heard of Baroness pudding ?

DANDINI (*absent-mindedly*).   Pleased to eat you.   (*He bows.*)

(*The* BARONESS, *in the background, bows too, but gets into difficulties with her panniers.*)

BARON.   We hope, Highness, that you were not inconvenienced by those two ruffians who were being chucked out ?

BARONESS.   Evicted, Oswald.

BARON.   Evicted.   We must apologise for the fracas.

(DANDINI *looks inquiringly at the* PRINCE, *who shrugs his shoulders, and indicates his ignorance of the word.   The* BARON *explains.*)

The rough house.

DANDINI (*looking up* R.).   Oh, the rough house.   Do you live there ?

BARON.   Er—we do, in a sense, sir, but we are thinking of leaving very shortly.

(*The* BARONESS *is still in difficulties with her panniers.*)

(*He looks at the* BARONESS.)   It is getting too small for us.   The two men whom you saw being chucked . . .

BARONESS.   Evicted !

BARON.   Exactly.   They—they—want to pinch . . .

BARONESS.   They have designs upon . . .

BARON.   Designs upon the furniture.

DANDINI.   Oh—furniture designers.

(*The* BARON *finds this funny and burst out laughing.*)

BARON.   That's right !   (*To the* BARONESS.)   My dear, the Prince has got a sense of humour.   Shall I tell him that one about . . .

BARONESS.   Oswald—please remember there is a *lady* present.   (*Aside to the* BARON.)   Call my daughters, quickly.   This is a chance not to be missed.

(*The* BARON *moves to the entrance up* R., *looks off and calls.*)

BARON (*calling*).   Bluebelle !   Maybelle !

(BLUEBELLE *and* MAYBELLE *enter down* L.)

BLUEBELLE ⎱ (*together*).   Here we are, Pa !
MAYBELLE ⎰

BARONESS.   You naughty girls—what do you mean by going out *alone*—without a chaperon ?

BLUEBELLE ⎱ (*together*).   Oh, Ma, we missed him !
MAYBELLE ⎰

BARONESS.   Missed who ?

BARON.   Missed *whom*, you mean.

(*The* BARONESS *gives the* BARON *a nasty look.*)

BLUEBELLE.   We missed the Prince.

MAYBELLE.   What a bore.

BARONESS (*trying to silence them*).   Sh !   Pull yourselves together.   The Prince is here.

(*The sisters catch sight of the* PRINCE *and* DANDINI, *talking together, and become suddenly confused.*)

BLUEBELLE ⎱ (*together*).   This is so sudden.
MAYBELLE ⎰

BARON (*moving* R.C.).   Wait for it.

BARONESS (*to* DANDINI).   These are my daughters, your Highness.   Bluebelle and Maybelle.

(*The* PRINCE *and* DANDINI *move a little down* C.)

BARON.   The Belles of the village—if I may be allowed to *chime* in—although I say it as shouldn't.

BARONESS.   You shertainly shouldn't !

BARON.   Your plate has got loose again, my dear !

(BLUEBELLE *and* MAYBELLE *cross below the* BARONESS *to* L.C. *and curtsey to* DANDINI *and the* PRINCE. *They are hampered by their gowns.*)

BLUEBELLE (*aside to the* BARONESS ; *agitatedly*).   Do we have to walk away backwards, Ma ?

(DANDINI *turns and whispers to the* PRINCE.)

BARONESS.   If you can.

(BLUEBELLE *and* MAYBELLE *attempt to walk backwards, and fall over.* CINDERELLA *enters down* L. *She wears a ragged dress. She carries a basket and a bundle of twigs.*)

DANDINI (*turning*).   There is no need to walk backwards.

BARON. Too late.

(BLUEBELLE *and* MAYBELLE *scramble to their feet, see* CINDERELLA, *and vent their wrath on her.*)

BLUEBELLE. Who are *you* staring at, pray ?

(*The* PRINCE *stares at* CINDERELLA *and points her out to* DANDINI.)

MAYBELLE. Go back to your kitchen.

(CINDERELLA *runs across below the* PRINCE *and* DANDINI, *and exits up* R.)

DANDINI. And who may she be ?

BARONESS. Only the kitchen maid.

PRINCE. *Only* the kitchen maid. (*Aside to* DANDINI.) I think I'll pay a visit to that kitchen. (*He moves up* R.)

BARON. Where are *you* off to, young man ?

PRINCE. I—I'm—feeling thirsty—I think I'll get a glass of water from your kitchen.

BARON. That's all you *will* get—in our kitchen.

(*The* PRINCE *exits up* R.)

BARONESS (*to* DANDINI). I'm sorry, your Highness, that we have nothing to offer you in the way of refreshment. The (*she mentions the name of a local wine merchant*) did not call this morning.

DANDINI. Don't let that worry you, madam. The hunt breakfast is being served, and if you and your charming family would care to take—pot-luck—shall we say . . .

(BLUEBELLE *and* MAYBELLE *smirk and curtsey.*)

BARON. Anything out of a *pot* will suit me. (*He holds up an imaginary tankard and smacks his lips.*)

DANDINI. My servant will bring refreshments here—if you do not mind alfresco eating.

(*They all bow as* DANDINI *exits up* L. *After his exit there is a pause while they look at each other.*)

BARONESS (*moving* R.). Who is Alf Resco ?

BARON. Sounds like a band leader.

BLUEBELLE (*facing front ; with a reminiscent expression*). Alf Resco and His Boys.

MAYBELLE (*clapping her hands delightedly*). Are we going to have a band as well as a beano ?

(BUTTONS *enters up* L. *to music. He carries two picnic baskets, one containing food, the other drink.*)

BUTTONS (*as he enters*). Here we are—the old firm, the old firm. (*He puts the baskets down up* C. *and moves down* C.)

(*The* BARON *and* BARONESS *are* R. *of* BUTTONS, BLUEBELLE *and* MAYBELLE L. *of him.*)

BLUEBELLE. Why, it's Buttons !

MAYBELLE. Buttons—come back again !

BARONESS (*struggling for words*). Buttons !

BARON. Well—dash my buttons—if it isn't Buttons !

BUTTONS. Yes—I'm Buttons all right—but not *your* **Buttons** now, Baron. I'm working for the Prince—up at the Castle.

BARON. Deserting the old ship, eh ?

BUTTONS. I've got into a new set.

BARON. A new set of buttons, eh ?

BUTTONS. Yes—and that's more than I ever got in your service.

BARON (*groaning*). Off with the old buttons—on with the new.

BLUEBELLE. Why didn't you ask pa for a rise ?

BARON (*tickled to death*). Tell her why you didn't ask me for a rise.

BUTTONS. If I'd asked *him* for a rise (*he jerks his thumb at the* BARON) he would have introduced his bootmaker to my tailor—see ?

MAYBELLE   ⎱ (*after trying to think it out ; together*). No—
BLUEBELLE   ⎰ —we're afraid we don't.

BUTTONS. In plain language—he'd have kicked me down the apples and pears.

MAYBELLE   ⎱ (*together*). We still don't !
BLUEBELLE   ⎰

BUTTONS (*giving it up*). Never mind—skip it ! (*He moves up* C. *and picks up the baskets.*)

BARONESS (*aghast*). Skip it ?

BARON (*with a sense of injury*). Skip the apples and pears ! We haven't had the first course, yet. What have you got to eat in those baskets ?

(BUTTONS *brings the baskets down* C.)

BUTTONS. How would you like it ? Tarble Dotty ?

BARON (*with a gesture*). No tarble !

BUTTONS. Then you'll have to have it *à la cart.*

BARON (*gesturing again*).   No cart !

BUTTONS.   All right—have a sandwich.   (*He produces some large square-cut sandwiches and hands them round.*)   There's one each.

BLUEBELLE.   What about Alf ?

BUTTONS.   Alf who ?

MAYBELLE.   Alf Resco.

BUTTONS.   If Alf turns up he'll have to go without. (*To the* BARONESS.)   Have a round ?

BARONESS (*taking a sandwich*).   This is not a round—it's a square.

BUTTONS (*grinning*).   A *square* meal in every *round*.

MAYBELLE.   Then—there are his Boys.

BUTTONS.   Whose boys ?

BLUEBELLE.   Alf's Boys.

BUTTONS (*getting upset*).   I'm not feeding the army, you know.

BARONESS (*in trouble with her sandwich*).   If you *were*, there'd be some complaints.   (*She holds the sandwich edge downwards.*)

BUTTONS.   They're not for eating.

BARONESS.   What *are* they for, then ?

BUTTONS (*looking around cautiously for eavesdroppers*).   They're for export.   And don't hold it like that.   (*He snatches the sandwich from the* BARONESS.)   You'll lose all the sawdust.   (*He puts the sandwiches back in the basket.*)

OMNES (*wiping their mouths*).   We've enjoyed that little snack.

BUTTONS.   Perhaps you'd like something a little more expensive. (*He produces a prop chicken from the basket.*)

BARONESS.   And what d'you call that ?

BUTTONS.   The chef's own suggestion—Larded Capon.

BLUEBELLE
MAYBELLE } (*together*).   La di da !

BARONESS (*suspiciously*).   And where did you get the lard ?

BUTTONS.   The Prince grows his own.   (*He replaces the chicken in the basket.*)

BARON.   He's putting on weight—and talking about weight— I'm still waiting.

BARONESS.   What for, Oswald ?

BARON (*as if he were addressing a public meeting*).   The reason for which this meeting was called, if I remember rightly, was to partake of liquid refreshment.   I would therefore suggest that our late employee, or black-leg, (*all look at* BUTTONS' *legs*) should proceed to liquidate the assets—in other words—uncork the fruity.

BUTTONS (*producing a bottle*). I have here some very good barley-water.

BARON (*with disgust*). Barley-water !

BUTTONS. Yes, barley-water. The Prince never drinks when out hunting. His motto is, " One at a time ".

BARON. That's drinking !

BUTTONS. Ah, don't miss the point, sir. Not " one drink at a time "—" one fox at a time."

BARON. Oh, very subtle. Still, I wouldn't mind seeing a couple of foxes—if I'd *had* a couple.

(*Business is introduced here. Two dummy foxes, fashioned out of cardboard, are drawn across the stage L. to R. near the footlights, by cord and pulley operated from the wings. The BARON stares as they go by. No one else sees them.*)

BARON (*to the BARONESS*). Did you—did you—s-see anything go by ?

BARONESS (*emphatically*). I did not !

BARON (*to BUTTONS*). Did you ?

BUTTONS. No. (*He takes a glass from the basket.*)

BLUEBELLE. What's the matter, Pa ?

MAYBELLE. Have you seen a spook ?

BARON (*muttering*). But—I *haven't* had a couple. (*To BUTTONS.*) I'll have some of that barley-water.

(BUTTONS *pours some out and passes the glass to the* BARON, *who takes it with a shaking hand and is about to drink when two* HUNTSMEN *run on down* L. *They hurry across to the* BARON.)

HUNTSMAN. Have you seen the fox ?

BARON (*firmly*). I have not !

(*The* HUNTSMEN *run past him to* R.)

(*He calls.*) Hi, you !

(*The* HUNTSMEN *stop and turn.*)

I haven't seen Alf, either.

HUNTSMAN. Alf who ?

BARON. Alf Resco.

(*The* HUNTSMEN *look at each other, then at the* BARON, *tap their heads significantly, wink and exit down* R. *The* PRINCE *enters up* R. *The* BARON *hands the glass to* BUTTONS, *who puts it in the basket along with the bottle, picks up the baskets, and exits up* L.)

B

BARONESS (*to the* PRINCE). Well, young man—have you had your drink of water ?

PRINCE (*moving* C.). I thank you, Baroness, I have had a most refreshing time. And that reminds me—the Prince is giving a ball at the Castle . . .

(DANDINI *enters up* L.)

I was just saying, your Highness, that you were giving a ball . . .

DANDINI (*forgetting his role*). Am I ?

PRINCE. Yes, of course you are. (*Aside to* DANDINI. *He nudges him.*) Play up, you fool.

DANDINI (*recovering*). Oh yes, of course you are. (*He corrects himself.*) Of—of—course I am.

PRINCE. His Highness requests the pleasure of the company of the Baron, Baroness and—*all* her charming daughters at the ball. Until then, he wishes you all adieu.

(DANDINI *bows and moves to the exit up* L., *followed by the* PRINCE. CINDERELLA *enters up* R., *and stands with her hands clasped, gazing at the* PRINCE *who sees her and gives her a smile, which the others do not see, as he exits with* DANDINI *up* L. CINDERELLA *runs to the exit up* L. *and stands gazing off as the music starts for the finale.*)

BARON (*to the* BARONESS). There you are, my dear—don't say I never introduce you to the right people.

BARONESS (*squashing him*). What had *you* to do with it ? For years I've worked and waited for this moment. At the Prince's Ball we shall meet the highest in the land. Bluebelle !

BLUEBELLE. Yes, Ma ?

BARONESS. Maybelle !

MAYBELLE. Yes, Ma ?

BARONESS. Now's your chance to get yourselves husbands. See that you pick good ones or I shall not give my approval.

(CINDERELLA *moves down* L.C.)

BARONESS. What are you doing here, Cinderella ?

CINDERELLA. I have been asked to the ball, too.

BLUEBELLE (*outraged*). *You* asked to the ball !

BARON. That's right enough. The Prince did say *all* the daughters.

MAYBELLE. And what is she going to wear ?

CINDERELLA.   But—Mother—I—I have been asked—the Prince . . .

BARONESS (*cutting in ; roughly*).   I cannot afford to send *three* daughters to the ball.   Besides, there is no necessity for *you* to get a husband.   You have your work in the kitchen.   You must give way to your elders and betters.

BLUEBELLE.   I should think so !

MAYBELLE.   We don't want the family disgraced.

BARONESS.   You mustn't be selfish.

CINDERELLA.   Selfish !   Oh !   (*She breaks down and with her hands to her face, moves up* R.)

(*The sound of a hunting horn is heard off* L.   BLUEBELLE *and* MAYBELLE *run up* C. *and look off* L.)

BLUEBELLE.   Here come the huntsmen.

The orchestra plays the theme for the finale.   The HUNTSMEN *enter with their partners for the final chorus.   The Principals give them the stage.   At the end of the number,* CINDERELLA *is seen, framed in the entrance up* R.   *She turns away from the merry-makers with her hands to her face as—*

the CURTAIN *falls.*

SCENE 2

SCENE.—*A street in the village.*

This is a comic interlude to give time for the change of scene.   It can be played on the apron or on a quarter stage.   The backcloth represents a street scene with a shop-front painted R.C.   *Over the shop is a large nameplate, "* GENERAL STORES.*"   A bell-rope hangs beside the shop door.   The shop window is practica and can be opened.*

When the CURTAIN *rises the stage is empty, then* COP *enters* L.   *He wheels a pram which contains a large bundle of washing.   Under the bundle and unseen by the audience are two rag-dolls representing babies.   They are exactly similar except that one has a black face and the other a white face.   As* COP *gets to* C., *the* WATCHMAN *enters* L. *and calls after him.*

WATCHMAN (*calling*).   Hi, you !

(COP *stops and turns.*)

What have you got in there ?

COP.   Only the washing—and the baby.

WATCHMAN (*suspiciously*).   Whose baby ?   (*He comes to* R. *of the pram.*)

COP.   *My* baby, you twerp !

WATCHMAN.   I'm not a twerp.

COP.   Yes you are—asking me whose baby.   You don't think I'd be carting someone else's baby, do you ?

WATCHMAN (*examining the pram*).   Where *is* the baby, anyway ?

COP.   Under the washing.

WATCHMAN.   *Under* the washing ?

COP.   My wife asked me to take the washing to the laundry and the baby for an airing—so I'm killing two birds with one stone, see ?

WATCHMAN.   You're doing the killing right enough.   Why don't you put the baby on top of the washing ?

COP.   Don't be silly—it would fall off.   It would get wet, too, if it rained.

WATCHMAN.   It's not going to rain.

COP.   How do *you* know ?

WATCHMAN.   Fancy putting all this on top of a poor little baby. (*He lifts off the bundle and looks inside the pram.*)   I *thought* so ! It's been suffocated !

COP.   Don't talk silly.

WATCHMAN (*holding the black-faced baby up in view of the audience*).   It's gone black in the face, anyway.

COP (*snatching the baby and putting it back in the pram*).   What are *you* doing—messing my baby about ?   Why don't you mind your own business ?

(SPY *enters* L. *and starts watching.*)

WATCHMAN.   It *is* my business.   I'm the Watch.

COP.   Go and watch somebody else for a change.

SPY (*moving* C.).   What's the trouble ?

WATCHMAN (*to* SPY).   I shall report him to the R.S.P.C.C.

SPY.   What for ?   (*He moves above the pram and peers into it.*)

WATCHMAN.   Baby-killing.

COP (*to the* WATCHMAN).   And I shall report you to Scotland Yard.

WATCHMAN.   What for ?

Cop.   Baby-*snatching*.

Spy.   I don't see anything wrong with the baby.

Watchman (*shouting*).   It's gone black in the face, I tell you !

Spy (*holding up the white-faced baby*).   You're a liar !

Watchman (*amazed ; scratching his head*).   Well—I'm a Dutchman !

Cop (*shouting*).   Go back to Holland.   Scram !   It only wanted a little air.   (*He snatches the baby from* Spy.)

Spy.   The air at (*he makes a local gag*) is very bracing.

Watchman (*moving* R. *with a puzzled expression*).   I didn't know it was as bracing as all that.

(*He exits* R.)

Cop.   I'll give it a little more 'air.   (*He takes a wig from the pram, claps it on the baby's head and puts the baby back in the pram.*)

Spy (R. *of the pram*).   Now Cop, you ought to be ashamed of yourself—playing the nursemaid when there's important work to be done.   How are we to get back to the Baron's house ?   Have you thought out any more schemes ?

Cop.   There's only one thing we can do now.

Spy.   What's that ?

Cop.   They've used force on us—we shall have to use force on them.   We shall have to be ruthless.   (*He suits the action to the word by replacing the washing on top of the babies in the pram.*)

Spy.   What's the plan ?

Cop.   We shall have to call out the military.

Spy.   How do we do that ?

Cop.   First of all, we must find out where the barracks is.

Spy.   Where the barracks are.

Cop.   Where the barracks *is*.

Spy.   Where the barracks *are*.   If you don't speak the King's English, you won't get the help of the King's Forces.

(*Arrange for someone in the audience to applaud this remark by clapping.* Spy *raises his hat and says :* " *Thank you both.*"   *An attractive* Girl *enters* L. *and crosses below* Cop *and* Spy *to* R.)

Cop.   There's a pedestrian.   Ask her where the barracks is.

Spy (*accosting the* Girl).   Excuse me, miss—can you tell us where the barracks— (*he hesitates*) can you tell us the way to the barracks ?

Girl.   I'm afraid not.   I'm a stranger.

Cop (*pushing forward*).   We can soon change all that.

SPY (*pushing* COP *away*). Behave yourself, Cop.

GIRL (*with a glance at the name over the shop ; innocently*) Why don't you ask General Stores ?

(*She turns and exits down* R. *As she does so, a rough-looking* PEDESTRIAN *enters* L. *and crosses to* R.)

SPY (*to the* PEDESTRIAN). Can you direct me to General Stores, please ?

PEDESTRIAN. Where ?

SPY. General Stores.

(*The* PEDESTRIAN *looks at the shop notice, then at* SPY. *His face hardens.*)

PEDESTRIAN. Now I'll ask *you* one. (*He points to the notice.*) Can't you read ?

(*He exits* R. SPY *and* COP *see the notice for the first time.*)

COP. Blimey ! We're there ! Now, you look after the family and I'll make inquiries.

(*While* COP *approaches the shop door,* SPY *wheels the pram* R.C. COP *pulls the bell-rope. There is a loud and prolonged ringing offstage. This can be done with hand-bells, the louder the funnier.* COP *and* SPY *put their fingers in their ears until the noise stops. The shop window opens suddenly and a* WOMAN'S *head appears.*)

WOMAN (*annoyed*). Was that you ringing ?

COP (*equally annoyed*). Not me. It's coming from *your* side. Are you selling muffins ?

WOMAN. We're closed. (*She bangs the window down.*)

COP (*moving* R. *to* SPY). They're closed.

SPY. You should have asked for the General.

COP. I didn't get a chance.

SPY. You asked for muffins. What for ? We don't want any muffins. Go back and ask to see the General.

(COP *returns to the shop and pulls the bell-rope again. Repeat the business of hand-bells, etc. The window opens again and the* WOMAN'S *head appears.*)

WOMAN. If you ring that bell again, I'll come out and wring your neck.

COP. We want to see the General.

WOMAN. General ? What General ?

Cop. General Stores.

Woman (*not understanding*). We've sold out. (*She bangs down the window.*)

Cop (*moving* R. *to* Spy). They're sold out of generals.

(*A fierce-looking* Recruiting Sergeant *enters* L. *and moves to* L. *of* Spy *and* Cop.)

Spy. Here's a sergeant. He'll know. Hey, sergeant. We're looking for the barracks. Can you take us there?

Sergeant (*looking pleased*). Can I take you to the barracks? Of course I can take you to the barracks.

Spy. That's very good of you.

Sergeant (*affably*). Not at all! That's what I'm paid for. (*He feels in his pocket and brings out two coins. He hands one to* Spy *and the other to* Cop.) There's a shilling for you—and a shilling for you.

Cop (*taking the shilling reluctantly*). Thank you, sergeant—but—we ought to be tipping *you* for your trouble.

Sergeant. Oh, that's not the drill. *You* take the shilling, and *we* do the rest. Off we go to the barracks. (*He takes them firmly by the arm, one on each side, and propels them towards the exit* R.)

Spy (*beginning to struggle*). But—we don't want to join up, you know.

Sergeant (*firmly*). You should have thought of that before you took the shilling, my lad.

Cop (*trying to free himself*). We want to see the General.

Sergeant (*roaring with laughter*). You'll see the General, all right. He'll be delighted to see *you*.

(*As the* Sergeant *hustles* Cop *and* Spy *off amid loud protests,* R., *the* Watchman *passes them, as he enters* R. *He looks after them for a moment, then his eyes fall on the unattended pram. He walks to it, lifts up the bundle, picks out the black-faced baby and holds it up.*)

Watchman. I thought so! Suffocated again! Not only suffocation, but desertion. I shall have to report this. (*He moves* C.)

(*A* Woman *enters* L., *recognises her pram, and gives the* Watchman *an angry look.*)

Woman (*moving* C.). What are you doing with my pram?

Watchman (*relieved*). Oh, it's your pram, is it?

WOMAN. Where's my husband ?

WATCHMAN (*jerking his head towards the exit* R.). Gone for a soldier !

WOMAN (*shrieking*). What ! (*She crosses to* R.)

WATCHMAN. I shall have to report you for cruelty to this poor baby. (*He holds up the black-faced baby.*)

WOMAN (*moving to the pram*). That's not my baby. (*She lifts the white-faced baby out of the pram, re-arranges the bundle and puts the baby back in a comfortable position. She wheels the pram to the exit* R. *and turns.*) You're a cuckoo, you are !

(*She exits* R. *as the lights black-out on the* WATCHMAN, *who stands* C. *and looks with a pained expression at the black-faced baby in his arms.*)

CURTAIN.

SCENE 3

SCENE.—*The* BARON'S *kitchen.*

> *A full stage is required for this scene. There are wide exits to the sides up* R. *and up* L. *to allow for the passage of whatever means of transport are used for taking* CINDERELLA *to the ball. There is a large ingle-nook fireplace* R., *which contains a masked exit. There is a door down* L. *The kitchen can have furnishings and properties as desired, but must include a table and chair* R.C. *and a stool by the chimney-corner.*

When the CURTAIN *rises the stage is empty, and* BLUEBELLE *is heard off* L., *calling.*

BLUEBELLE (*off* L. ; *calling*). Cinderella.

(BLUEBELLE *enters up* L. *She is half-dressed, in her corsets, and with her hair in curlers. She carries a new gown over her arm. While waiting for the laughter her ridiculous appearance should get, to subside, she looks around the stage for* CINDERELLA.)

(*She calls.*) Cinderella. Come here at once. Drat the girl—where has she gone to. (*She calls.*) *Cinderella !*

MAYBELLE (*off* L. ; *calling*). *Cinderella !*

BLUEBELLE (*calling*). Cinderella !

MAYBELLE (*off* L. ; *calling*). Cinderella !

(The intention here is for BLUEBELLE *to give the impression that she has heard an echo.* MAYBELLE *enters up* L. *She is similarly half-dressed and also carries a new gown over her arm.)*

BLUEBELLE.   Oh, it's you !

MAYBELLE.   Oh, it's you !

BLUEBELLE.   Don't mock me, Maybelle.

MAYBELLE.   I'm looking for Cinderella.

BLUEBELLE.   So am I.   I want some help with this gown.   I want to see what I look like.

MAYBELLE.   So do I.   But *I* can tell you what you'll look like —you'll look a little *passée.*

BLUEBELLE.   What !

MAYBELLE.   Well—you *are* two years older than me, aren't you ?   Two years is a lot you know, when it comes to getting a man.

BLUEBELLE *(thinking hard for some counter-blow).*   Experience counts.

MAYBELLE *(staring at her wide-eyed).*   And when did you pick *that* up, may I ask ?

BLUEBELLE *(evasively).*   Never you mind.

(There is a loud knock on the door down L.*)*

(She calls.)   Come in !

(The WATCHMAN *enters down* L. *He carries the black-faced baby as if very anxious to get rid of it.)*

WATCHMAN.   I've brought this baby . . .

BLUEBELLE *(moving to him).*   Well, you can take it away again. *We* don't want it.

WATCHMAN *(desperately).*   Let me explain . . .

BLUEBELLE *(pushing him away).*   We don't want any babies.

WATCHMAN.   I'm the watchman and I . . .

BLUEBELLE.   We don't want any watches, either.   Nothing to-day, thank you.

(The WATCHMAN *is hustled off down* L. *and* BLUEBELLE *shuts the door.   The* BARON *enters up* L. *He is also half-dressed and carries a cravat in his hand.* MAYBELLE *eases* R.C.*)*

BARON *(moving* C.*).*   What's all the argument about ?

BLUEBELLE *(*L. *of the* BARON*).*   A man selling babies.   *(In a matter-of-fact tone.)*   I told him we didn't want any.   Where's Cinderella, Pa ?

It's so unfair, why can everyone go out and have fun and I have to stay in and work. If only I could be there too! (cry — G-Mother appears. + sing)

BARON (*looking around*).   Isn't she here?

MAYBELLE (R. *of the* BARON).   She's *never* here when she's wanted.   I don't know what's come over the girl lately.   Pa, you'll have to give her a good talking to.

BARON.   Perhaps she's gone upstairs.

BLUEBELLE (*shortly*).   She hasn't gone upstairs.

BARON (*trying to be helpful*).   Perhaps she's gone up the chimney.

MAYBELLE.   Pa, don't be ridiculous.

BLUEBELLE (*contemptuously*).   How could she go up the chimney?

BARON.   She might have gone up in smoke.

MAYBELLE.   Pa, you really are impossible.

BARON.   You complain about having a dull father and when I *do* say something witty, you say I'm impossible.

BLUEBELLE (*holding up her gown*).   What d'you think of my new dress, Pa?

BARON.   That ought to fetch 'em.

MAYBELLE (*holding up hers*).   And what d'you think of mine?

BARON.   That ought to knock 'em cold.

BLUEBELLE.   Which do you like best, Pa?

BARON (*not to be caught*).   As I'm supposed to be impossible—*both*.   Now, go upstairs, put 'em on and then ask your mother.   She knows all the right answers.   Here—help me on with my cravat, will you?

BLUEBELLE (*moving up* L.).   You can ask Cinderella to do that.

MAYBELLE (*moving up* L.).   We know she'll do anything for *you*.

(*They exit up* L.)

BARON (*calling*).   Cinderella!

(CINDERELLA *enters up* R.)

Now where have you been hiding yourself?

CINDERELLA (*moving to* R. *of the* BARON *at* C.).   I'll come when *you* call, Pa, but not when *they* call.   I've had enough of them. I'm on strike to-day.

BARON (*horrified*).   You can't do that, Cinderella.

CINDERELLA.   Put me in prison, then.   I couldn't be *worse* off.

BARON (*kindly*).   You mustn't talk like that.   (*He hands her his cravat.*)

CINDERELLA.   Pa, why can't I go to the ball?   (*She puts his cravat on for him.*)

BARON. Don't start that again, Cinderella. Your mother says you haven't got a dress, so that's that. I'm sorry, my dear, but there it is. I'll smuggle something back for you, for a treat. An éclair, or a bath-bun or something.

CINDERELLA (*getting tearful*). I don't *want* a bath-bun.

BARON. Now don't cry over my one and only cravat, or *I* shan't be able to go to the ball either.

CINDERELLA (*sobbing*). It isn't fair.

BARON (*trying to comfort her*). I'll get you a new dress when my ship comes home.

(CINDERELLA *stops crying suddenly and looks interested.*)

CINDERELLA. I didn't know you had a ship.

BARON (*embarrassed*). Well—er—it's not—er—it's not *my* ship, really—but—I've got an interest in it, doncherknow. I know one of the stewards. We'll get you a new dress, don't worry, my dear —one of these days.

(*He exits up* L.)

CINDERELLA (*moving down* C.). One of these days ! What's the good of that ? I want it for to-night.

(CINDERELLA *can now have her first song. The song must match her sentimental mood. Therefore avoid a " snappy " number here. After the song she sits on the stool in the chimney-corner. The orchestra continues softly the theme of her song. She speaks through the music, indulging in a day-dream.*)

CINDERELLA. I shall never forget him—even if I never see him again. (*She looks towards the door down* L.) To think that he actually knocked at that door and came in and asked for a glass of water.

(*There is a knock at the door.*)

(*She rises with suppressed excitement and moves* C.) There it is again ! The same knock.

(*There is another knock at the door.*)

(*She turns slightly away from the door down* L., *clasps her hands tightly, shuts her eyes, takes a deep breath and calls.*) Come in.

(BUTTONS *enters down* L. *He carries a large flower concealed behind his back, and creeps up behind* CINDERELLA, *who maintains her pose.*)

BUTTONS. Hi, Cinders ! (*He throws his cap on to the table.*)

CINDERELLA (*turning ; startled*). Oh, Buttons !

BUTTONS. I thought you'd gone into a trance.

CINDERELLA (*rubbing her eyes*). I—I was just—thinking.

BUTTONS. Ah, you shouldn't do that, Cinders—that's my job. I'm better at it than you. I did a lot of thinking to get here to see you.

CINDERELLA (*still preoccupied*). Did you, Buttons ?

BUTTONS. I certainly did. A rare old job I had to get away. But I thought you would be lonely and so . . . (*He pauses.*) Cinders—don't look so sad.

CINDERELLA. I'm not sad, Buttons. I was just wondering if . . .

BUTTONS. If I had deserted you ?

CINDERELLA. Oh no ! I was—I was—j-just being soppy, that's all.

BUTTONS. *You* mustn't be soppy. *I'm* the soppy one now. Look what I've brought you, Cinders. (*He holds out the large flower which he has been concealing behind him.*)

CINDERELLA (*taking the flower*). Oh, Buttons, what a lovely flower ! (*She turns away from him and buries her nose in the flower.*)

(BUTTONS *waits expectantly to be thanked, but she keeps her back to him. There is a pause.*)

BUTTONS (*breaking the awkward silence*). Yes, that's a good flower—a very expensive flower, that is. That's from the Prince's garden.

CINDERELLA (*turning to him ; eagerly*). Did the Prince give it to you ?

BUTTONS. Give it to *me* ? Course he didn't give it to me. Now, would he give *me* flowers ?

CINDERELLA. I thought perhaps . . .

BUTTONS. Now you're *thinking* again. I picked it myself.

(CINDERELLA *turns away again.*)

Now you're looking sad again.

(*There is another awkward pause.*)

I had to go through a lot to get that flower. I had **four gardeners** chasing me. (*He pauses.*) Nearly lost my job.

(CINDERELLA *relents and turns to him.*)

(*He puts his arm around her and grins.*)　That's more like the old Cinders.

(CINDERELLA *gets tearful again.*)

Come and have a good cry on the Cain and Abel.

(*He helps her to the table* R.C.　*They sit on it.*)

CINDERELLA.　I'm not the old Cinders any more, Buttons. I've changed.

BUTTONS.　Changed ?　When ?

CINDERELLA (*dreamily*).　Ever since someone came in here and asked me for a glass of water.

BUTTONS (*mystified*).　Glass of water ?

CINDERELLA.　Yes.

BUTTONS.　Who was that—some old tramp ?

CINDERELLA.　Tramp !　He was beautifully dressed and looked so handsome.

(BUTTONS *jumps off the table.*)

BUTTONS.　Now don't get ideas above your station, Cinders.

CINDERELLA.　He gave me such a lovely smile.

BUTTONS.　Course he did !　That's his job.　They don't mean anything when they smile.　Now—when *I* smile . . .

CINDERELLA (*obstinately*).　He *did* mean something.　I'm sure he did.　Oh, I wish I could go to the ball.

BUTTONS (*fed up*).　Still thinking about that silly old ball.　You wouldn't enjoy it if you did go.

CINDERELLA.　Oh, Buttons, think of it.　All the bright lights and the lovely dresses and the gay music.

BUTTONS.　And the people treading on your pet corn and dropping ice-cream down your back, and jabbering a lot of silly nonsense.　(*He imitates.*)　" My dear !　We're having a perfectly wonderful time ! "　" Hello, Lady Ermintrude, and how's the dear Duke ? "　" Have you sold your new hunter, Sir John ? "　" Twy one of these sausage wolls, Margawet—they're wavishing ! "　(*He goes to* CINDERELLA, *still imitating.*)　" Cindewella—may I have the pleasure of a dance ? "

(CINDERELLA *laughs, catches his mood, and they have a dance together. This can be extended into a full song and dance number, if desired. After the number,* BUTTONS *escorts* CINDERELLA *to the stool with exaggerated ceremony.*)

Did you enjoy that dance, Cinders ?

CINDERELLA (*sitting on the stool*). Yes, Buttons. It was lovely.

BUTTONS. I didn't tread on your pet corn, did I ?

CINDERELLA. No, Buttons.

BUTTONS. And I didn't drop any ice-cream down your back, did I ?

CINDERELLA. No, Buttons.

BUTTONS. So—do you still want to go to the ball ?

CINDERELLA (*gazing up at him with an innocent look*). Yes, Buttons.

(BUTTONS *picks up his cap from the table, flings the cap on to the floor and stamps on it.*)

Buttons !

BUTTONS (*exasperated*). It's no good trying to understand women. They just don't make sense.

CINDERELLA. I'm sorry, Buttons.

BUTTONS (*calming down*). I'm sorry, too, Cinders. I'm sorrier than I've ever been. I can see I haven't got a chance with these fine gentlemen knocking around and asking for glasses of water. There's only one thing *I'd* ask you for, Cinders, but I've got a feeling you'd—you'd say—no.

CINDERELLA (*rising and moving to him*). Buttons, I'm—I'm very fond of you and I don't know what I should do without you and I'll always . . .

BUTTONS. *Be a sister to me*—I know—you needn't say it. But you won't get me to call *you* sister, Cinders. (*He picks up his cap.*) I must go now, but—I shall come back again—and I shall go on coming back—as long as there's a blinkin' flower left in the blinkin' Prince's blinkin' garden.

(*Overcome by his emotion, he hurries to the door down L. and exits without looking back.* CINDERELLA, *sorry for him, runs impulsively to the door down L., and opens it. As she does so, the* FAIRY GODMOTHER *enters down R. and stands down R. watching. She wears a cloak and high hat, and carries a stick.*)

CINDERELLA (*calling*). Buttons ! I didn't mean to be unkind. Buttons !

(*The* FAIRY GODMOTHER *chuckles.* CINDERELLA *turns quickly, sees her, and gives a cry of surprise.*)

GODMOTHER. It's no use calling for Buttons, Cinderella. He won't come back.

There's no use in crying noone can hear you.

after songs —

CINDERELLA (*moving* C.). ~~How you frightened me.~~ Who are you ? How did you get in ? What do you want ?

GODMOTHER. What a lot of questions for a poor old woman to answer. (*She chuckles again.*) Who am I ? Supposing I told you I was your Fairy Godmother ?

CINDERELLA (*with a gasp*). My Fairy Godmother !

GODMOTHER. How did I get in ? That's an easy one. I can get in anywhere. ~~I don't have to ring the front-door bell, you know.~~ I walked in the front door.

CINDERELLA. Why have you come ?

GODMOTHER. Another question ! You're on my books, Cinderella, and I've come to get you off. But—I've got a difficult job, haven't I ? That frock ! You can't go to the ball like that.

CINDERELLA. Please do not speak about the ball. (*She turns away.*) I don't want to be reminded of it.

GODMOTHER. Don't be silly, child. The ball is going to be one of your fondest memories.

CINDERELLA (*turning*). You're teasing !

GODMOTHER (*sternly*). Cinderella—come here.

(CINDERELLA, *as if impelled against her will, approaches the* FAIRY GODMOTHER, *who turns to her so that her face is hidden from the audience.*)

Look at me !

(CINDERELLA *looks at the* FAIRY GODMOTHER, *gives a little gasp, and turns away.*)

CINDERELLA. You have such strange eyes.

GODMOTHER. Do I look as if I would tease you ?

CINDERELLA (*as if in a trance*). No.

GODMOTHER. Then—do as I tell you. Go back to your chimney corner and sit down. Something very strange is going to happen to you, but—don't be frightened—it won't hurt.

(CINDERELLA *moves to the stool by the chimney-corner and sits.*)

Don't worry—just sit back and relax. *quietly* *don't worry*

(*The lights start to dim out.*)

Just let yourself go—slowly—slowly . . .

(*As the lights dim to black-out, the voice of the* FAIRY GODMOTHER *fades out, and in the darkness, she exits up* R. *Also during the*

duet ⇒ I will survive

looka like
ballet & fairies

darkness, CINDERELLA *exits quickly through the fireplace and her place on the stool is taken by a double who sits with her face turned from the audience during the ensuing* ballet. CINDERELLA *meanwhile effects a quick change into her ball-dress. After a few moments the lights come up and a Fairy Ballet follows. On the last bars of their dance, the fairies make a masking movement around the fireplace, the double exits, and* CINDERELLA *resumes her seat on the stool. When the dance finishes, the fairies dress the stage* R. *and* L., *the* FAIRY GODMOTHER *enters up* R., *and* CINDERELLA *rises and moves* C.)

GODMOTHER (*moving down* C.). Now—let's have a look at you. (*She surveys* CINDERELLA.) Yes—you'll do. If I don't get you off my books in *that* creation, I'll give up magic and go back to my chars.

CINDERELLA. Oh, Fairy Godmother—am I really going to the ball ?

GODMOTHER. Of course you're going to the ball. What do you think I've dressed you up like a wedding-cake for ? And there's *going* to be a wedding *too*, if I'm not mistaken.

CINDERELLA. Now you *are* teasing.

GODMOTHER (*with a chuckle*). Perhaps I am, this time. But—it's up to you. Now I've only one more thing to say and it's very important, Cinderella, so stop admiring yourself and listen. That beautiful dress does not belong to you, remember that. You must not tear it and, after twelve o'clock, you must not wear it. Indeed, you will not be able to wear it because it will be taken from you and you will find yourself once more in your working clothes. So—don't forget—at twelve o'clock you must hasten from the ballroom and get back here as quick as you can or you will spoil all your chances. Is that clear ?

CINDERELLA. Yes, Fairy Godmother. I will do all that you tell me. But—how am I to *get* to the ball ?

GODMOTHER. Don't worry about that. It has been arranged for you by the fairies. See !

At a gesture from the FAIRY GODMOTHER, *a sedan-chair is carried on by two chairmen. The chair is richly decorated and illuminated. The music starts for the finale.* CINDERELLA *steps into the chair and is borne off, escorted by the fairies as—*

the CURTAIN *falls.*

NOTE.—*These directions are only a suggestion. The transport arrangements for taking* CINDERELLA *to the ball will, of course, depend on the limitations of the stage and materials available. Producers are therefore left to make their own arrangements if they so desire.*

SCENE 4

SCENE.—*Outside the castle.*

The scene is a drop, with practical gates C. *to the castle, which is represented on the backcloth behind them.*

When the CURTAIN *rises, the gates are shut. The voice of the* SERGEANT *is heard shouting orders off* L. *After a moment,* COP *and* SPY, *followed by the* SERGEANT *enter* L. COP *and* SPY *wear the uniform of sentries and carry rifles. They march on out of step to* C., COP *leading.*

SERGEANT. Pick 'em up, there. Left, right, left, right. Halt ! About turn.

(SPY *and* COP *make a mess of it, but finish up facing* L., COP R. *of and behind* SPY.)

(*He surveys them with contempt.*) How am I going to make sentries out of two twerps like you ? You don't seem to have any idea of how to put one foot in front of the other. Ain't that easy enough ? What's the matter ? Have you got somebody else's feet to-day ?

(SPY *examines his own feet and appears to be satisfied.*)

SPY. I've got mine all right.
SERGEANT (*roaring*). Don't answer me back. Sentries ain't allowed to talk. Now—listen to me. (*He points off* R.) There's a sentry-box over there (*he points off* L.) and another sentry-box over there. You march up and down between those two boxes.
COP. What for ?
SERGEANT (*aghast*). What for ? Because you're on sentry-go. That's your beat.
COP (*aside to* SPY). Can you beat it ?
SERGEANT (*roaring*). No talking ! Now—let's see you go through the motions. (*To* COP.) About turn.

(SPY *and* COP *both turn about.*)

(*To* SPY.) Not you ! About turn.

C

(Spy *and* Cop *both turn about.*)

(*He howls with rage, moves to* Spy *and holds him as he gives the order again.*) About turn.

(Cop *turns about and now faces* R. *with his back to* Spy.)

(*He releases* Spy.) Quick march.

(Spy *marches off* L. *and* Cop *off* R.)

(*He calls after them as they exit.*) When you get to your box, about turn and march back.

(*There is a prolonged clattering off* R., *then* Cop *re-enters* R., *carrying a large bucket.*)

(*To* Cop.) What have you done now ?

Cop (*holding out the bucket*). Please Sergeant, this was on my beat.

Sergeant. You don't have to fall over it, do you ?

(Spy *enters* L. *and marches to* C.)

Some mothers do have 'em. Put that bucket down. (*He turns suddenly away from* Cop *and collides with* Spy.) Why don't you look where you're going ?

(Cop *puts the bucket on the ground behind him.*)

Spy (*with confidence*). You're on my beat.

(*The* Sergeant *stands between them and gives way to despair.*)

Sergeant. I've recruited a pair of lunatics. (*He suddenly shouts.*) Fall in !

(Cop, *startled, overbalances and sits in the bucket.*)

Not in the bucket. (*He points* R.C.) Fall in over there.

(Cop *rises, puts the bucket* R., *then he and* Spy *stand side by side,* Cop R. *of* Spy, *facing front.*)

Now—let me see if you know how to present arms. I want it done nicely.

Cop. I can do it nicely, Sergeant. Watch me. (*He goes down on one knee and holds out his rifle with a feminine gesture to the* Sergeant, *as if he were presenting him with a bouquet.*)

(*The* Sergeant *snatches* Cop's *rifle from him.*)

SERGEANT. I'll give you one more chance. *You* watch *me*, this time.

(He goes through the motions of presenting arms, then returns the rifle to COP *and puts them through the drill. He then marches them off* R. SPY *and* COP *carefully avoid the bucket, but the* SERGEANT, *intent on watching their steps, stumbles over it himself. As* SPY, COP *and the* SERGEANT *exit* R., *a party of sightseers enter* L. *They are led by a uniformed* GUIDE, *who carries a megaphone. The party can consist of any number of types, but dialogue and business has been provided in the text for the following : A Cockney family consisting of* WIFE, *her* HUSBAND, *who has a drooping moustache, their small* BOY *who sucks at a bottle of lemonade and* GRANDPA, *who wears dark glasses and carries an ear-trumpet and an umbrella. There is also a sour-looking, argumentative* MAN.)

GUIDE (*through the megaphone*). We have now arrived at the entrance to the castle.

MAN. You're telling us.

GUIDE (*stiffly*). That's my job, sir. (*Through the megaphone.*) I will now give you a short account of these historic surroundings. Will you all come closer, please.

(The party bunches around the GUIDE.)

MAN (*not liking it*). Ain't we close enough?

HUSBAND (*not liking it either*). I should have thought so.

BOY. Mum, what's he shouting through that grammerfone for?

WIFE. I expect he thinks we're a long way away.

HUSBAND. He ought to get some glasses.

MAN. So ought that boy of yours. He'll cut his mouth on that bottle if he's not careful.

WIFE. It's not *your* bottle, is it?

MAN. If it were, *I'd* get some glasses, too, and share it round. (*He mops his brow.*)

GUIDE (*discarding the megaphone*). You are now standing outside the Castle gates. These gates . . .

MAN. What are we waiting for?

HUSBAND (*bursting into the old song*). " Wot are we waiting for, Oh my heart. Kiss me straight on the brow." (*He laughs.*)

WIFE. Henry, do behave yourself. Albert, stop sucking that bottle. You'll make yourself sick.

HUSBAND (*to the* GUIDE ; *helpfully*). What he means is—wot are we standing *outside* for ? Why don't we go *inside* ?

GUIDE. The public are not allowed in to-day.

MAN. Why not ?

GUIDE. Because His Highness is in residence.

MAN. Bit selfish, ain't he ?

HUSBAND. His Nibs is quite right. *I* wouldn't allow people to walk about in *my* garden.

MAN. Oh, wouldn't you ?

HUSBAND. Not while I was in residence. Neither would you —if you *had* a garden—which I doubt.

MAN (*threateningly*). Who says I haven't got a garden ?

HUSBAND. I do—or you wouldn't be talking like that.

MAN. You want to be careful what you say.

WIFE. Stop it, you two. Why don't you listen to what the guide has to say—and *learn* something.

(*This silences the two men and the* GUIDE, *who has been patiently waiting to get a word in, resumes his speech.*)

GUIDE. Ladies and gentlemen . . .

WIFE. Albert—stop sucking that bottle. What will His Highness say if he comes out and sees you ?

GUIDE. If you will all turn round and face this way (*he points to the audience*) you will see a magnificent panorama.

(*Everyone faces front.*)

WIFE (*impressed with what she sees*). Well I never ! What did he say it was ?

HUSBAND. Panorama. (*He turns to* GRANDPA *and shouts into the ear-trumpet.*) Panorama.

(GRANDPA *looks bewildered.*)

WIFE. What's a panorama ?

HUSBAND. It's a basinful—if you know what I mean. (*He laughs, then shouts into* GRANDPA'S *ear-trumpet.*) Basinful.

(GRANDPA *looks more bewildered still.*)

GUIDE (*with a sweep of the arm in the direction of the audience*). A vista where—as the poet says—" every prospect pleases and only man is vile."

HUSBAND. Wot about woman ?

GUIDE. The poet didn't mention woman.

MAN. His wife wouldn't let him, that's why.

WIFE. How do *you* know ? Are you married ?

MAN. Not bloomin' likely !

WIFE. Then don't show yer ignorance.

HUSBAND. That's right—start another row.

GUIDE (*patiently carrying on*). A big battle was fought over this ground. Out there once charged, full tilt, hundreds of knights in armour.

HUSBAND. That accounts for the panorarmour.

GUIDE. Under your very feet lie dead men.

WIFE. Ow ! What sort of place have you brought me to ?

(*Everyone looks anxiously on the ground. The* BOY *starts roaming about.*)

HUSBAND. It was your idea, wasn't it ? I wanted to go to the pictures.

(*The* BOY *peers over the footlights.*)

WIFE. Albert ! Mind where you go. There's a big ditch there. (*She pulls him away from the footlights.*)

GUIDE. That's not a ditch, madam—that's a moat.

HUSBAND (*to the* GUIDE). She hasn't the *remotest* ! (*He laughs at his own pun, then shouts into* GRANDPA's *ear-trumpet.*) Did you hear that crack, Grandpa ?

GUIDE. The moat dried up a long time ago.

MAN. Pity you didn't.

GUIDE. The Castle was built in ten sixty-six.

HUSBAND (*into* GRANDPA's *ear-trumpet*). And all that !

GUIDE. During the Civil War it was very much knocked about —by Cromwell's men.

HUSBAND (*starting another song*). " I'm one of the ruins that Cromwell knocked about a bit."

WIFE. Henry, why don't you stop making a fool of yourself ? Nobody's laughing at you.

HUSBAND. Yes they are.

WIFE. Who is ?

HUSBAND. I am ! (*He laughs heartily.*)

WIFE. Henry, look what Albert's doing now. Stop him !

(*The* BOY, *who has been on the prowl again, is now behind* GRANDPA, *holding his bottle of lemonade tipped over the edge of the ear-trumpet which* GRANDPA *is holding to his ear. The* HUSBAND *gets hold of the* BOY *and in the struggle* GRANDPA *gets a drop of lemonade in his ear, thinks it is beginning to rain and puts up his umbrella.*)

HUSBAND.   All right, Grandpa, it's not raining.
GRANDPA.   I felt a spot.
MAN (*mopping his brow again*).   There's a difference between *feeling* a spot and *having* a spot.
GUIDE (*through the megaphone*).   Ladies and gentlemen !
MAN.   Put a sock in it !
GUIDE (*through the megaphone*).   Will you all please follow me and we will move on.

(*His voice is stopped by some old socks which the* MAN *stuffs down the megaphone. The* GUIDE, *pushed about with much good-natured laughter from the party in general, retires in a huff and exits* R. GRANDPA, *with his umbrella still up, retires upstage to the gates* C. *The* HUSBAND *follows him, gets under the umbrella and starts up another song.*)

HUSBAND (*singing*).   " In the shade of the old apple-tree."

(*The rest of the party gather round the umbrella and join in the singing. The* BARONESS, *followed by the* BARON, *enters* L. *They are dressed for the ball, under their travelling-cloaks. The singing fades out as they appear. The party should, however, keep up the fun, but subdued, so as not to drown the lines of the principals.*)

BARONESS.   Who are these vulgar people ?
BARON.   They sound to me like the waits.
BARONESS.   Tell them to *wait* elsewhere.   We can't wait, anyway.   It's raining and we shall spoil our clothes.
BARON (*looking up and holding out his hand*).   It's not raining, my love.
BARONESS.   It *is* raining.   That old man's holding up an umbrella.   I'm not blind, Oswald.   Go and tell them to stand clear of the gates.
BARON.   I can't do that, my dear.
BARONESS.   Why not ?
BARON.   They'll think I'm the lift-man.
BARONESS.   If you *were* the lift-man, you would at least be of *some* use.   (*She gives him a withering look.*)   I'll do it myself.   (*She approaches the party.*)   Stand clear of the gates.
HUSBAND.   Going up !   Third floor—ladies underwear.   (*He starts to sing.*)   " There was I, waiting at the church."

(The party join in enthusiastically. The BARONESS *makes an angry gesture and moves* L. *The* SERGEANT *enters* R. *and marches to* C.)

BARONESS.   Sergeant, will you please tell this rabble to move on.

HUSBAND (*aside*).   What a hope !

SERGEANT.   You want a policeman, madam.

BARONESS.   What's the matter with the army ?

SERGEANT.   Ah, now you're *asking* something. What's the matter with the army ? Perhaps you'd like to see for yourself. (*He blows his whistle.*)

HUSBAND.   Offside.

*(*SPY *and* COP *march on* R., *carrying their rifles the wrong way round.*)

SERGEANT.   Halt !   About turn !

*(*SPY *turns about and faces* COP, *who ignores the order.*)

That's what's the matter with the army, madam, and if you want a first-class headache, you can give 'em the orders yourself.

BARONESS.   I order them to charge the crowd.

COP (*eagerly*).   How much ?

SERGEANT (*with a groan*).   You see, madam, what *I've* had to put up with.

(The party start to sing " Pack up your troubles in your old kit-bag and smile, smile, smile." The SERGEANT *gives up the struggle and exits* R. *The* BARON, *unable to resist the fun, joins in the song.*)

BARONESS.   Oswald, how dare you !   Come away !

(The BARON *obeys with reluctance. The party has now got into its stride with community-singing. The* HUSBAND *conducts the choir with* GRANDPA's *umbrella ;* SPY *and* COP *produce collecting-boxes and " charge " all and sundry, including the audience, with " any little sum they might like to contribute." Local charities can be mentioned. During the business the* PRINCE, *disguised as* DANDINI, *enters* R. *and stands watching the proceedings. At the end of the song, the* HUSBAND *notices him.*)

HUSBAND.   Blimey !   Here's Gilbert the Filbert !

PRINCE (*entering into the spirit of the proceedings*).   Well sung, my livelies. (*He empties his purse on the ground.*)   Share that amongst you.

(As the coins roll about, the party break away to pick them up, and leave the gates free. The BARON *joins in the scramble for the coins, and succeeds in securing one or two. The* PRINCE *moves to the gates and opens them.)*

BARONESS. Now's our chance, Oswald. Follow me. (*She sweeps up to the gates.*)

(*The* PRINCE *holds the gates open for her.*)

She gives the PRINCE *a patronizing look.*) Thank you, my man.

She exits up C. *to* L. *The* BARON *moves to the gates and tips the* PRINCE *with the coins he has picked up.*)

PRINCE (*accepting the tip*). Thank you, sir.
BARON. Not at all !

As he exits up C. *to* L., *the lights black-out and—*

the CURTAIN *falls.*

ALTERNATIVE ENDING.

BARON. Not at all !

(*He exits up* C. *to* L.)

PRINCE. Now we've all got going, it seems a pity to break up the party. Here's a song we can *all* sing.

He sings a song in which he gets the audience to sing too, with the support of those still left on the stage. As the song finishes—

the CURTAIN *falls.*

SCENE 5

SCENE.—*The ballroom.*

The back of the stage is raised, and wide steps up C. *lead down from it. There are entrances* R. *and* L.

When the CURTAIN *rises, the* GUESTS *are dancing. As the dance finishes, the* HERALD *enters up* C., *and announces from the top of the steps.*)

HERALD. My lords and ladies—the Prince would like to take wine with his guests.

(*He exits up* C. *The* GUESTS *file out, laughing and chatting, to the last bars of the music.* BUTTONS *enters* L. *He carries a tray of drinks. He crosses from* L. *to* R. *As he does so,* DANDINI *enters up* C., *comes down the steps and intercepts him.*)

DANDINI. What have we here ?

BUTTONS. Specials for the Prince. Just as he likes it.

DANDINI. Just as *I* like it. (*He helps himself to a drink, tastes it, and smacks his lips.*) Very good. In fact, excellent.

BUTTONS (*who has been watching him with displeasure*). **How** long are you going to keep up this racket ?

DANDINI (*raising his eye-brows*). This—what, my dear Buttons ?

BUTTONS. Racket, I said. Pretending to be someone else.

DANDINI. It's good while it lasts. (*He tosses off the drink and looks at the empty glass.*) So's this. (*He takes another drink from the tray.*) Haven't you ever wanted to be someone else, Buttons ?

BUTTONS (*shortly*). No, I haven't.

DANDINI. Never wanted to play a part—to be an actor ?

BUTTONS. I don't like actors—they're humbugs.

DANDINI. But think of the glory of being Principal **Boy for** once. The lime-light ! The applause !

BUTTONS. I've thought of all that.

DANDINI. And you wouldn't like to be Principal Boy ?

BUTTONS (*with contempt*). It's a girl's job !

(DANDINI *shows embarrassment at this, but laughs it off.*)

DANDINI. What about Hamlet, then. He was a principal boy.

BUTTONS. I saw him once. I didn't think much of *him*.

DANDINI. You saw Hamlet ? In the play, you mean.

BUTTONS. *After* the play. He was in a café eating fish and chips.

(DANDINI *laughs.*)

(*Defensively.*) You've got to be yourself sometimes, you know.

DANDINI. Buttons, you're a cynic. (*He raises his glass.*) Here's to make-believe, fame and fortune. (*He drains his glass and puts it back on the tray.*)

BUTTONS. You can't take it with you !

DANDINI. Can't I ? Watch me !

(*He calmly takes the tray of drinks from the astonished* BUTTONS *and walks off with it* L. *As he goes, he passes the* BARON, *who enters* L. *Without looking up, the* BARON *mechanically takes a glass from the tray.*)

BARON. That's very nice of you.

(DANDINI *bows and exits* L. *On his way out, he passes* BLUEBELLE, MAYBELLE *and the* BARONESS, *who have followed the* BARON. *They register amazement at what they take to be the* PRINCE *handing round drinks himself.*)

BARONESS. Oswald, do you realize who that was ?

BARON. Didn't notice, my dear. Good Samaritan, anyway. Just what the doctor ordered—and no queueing. (*He drinks.*)

(BUTTONS *eases down* R.)

MAYBELLE. That was the *Prince*, Pa.

BLUEBELLE. Just like you, Pa.

BARONESS. Just when we wanted to make a good entrance.

BARON. Well, if that was His Royal Highness, what does he mean by handing round the drinks ?

BLUEBELLE. He *wasn't* handing them round. He was walking away with them.

BARON. That's worse ! We're thirsty—and we *are* the guests, you know.

BARONESS (*exasperated*). Why didn't you *look ?*

BARON. One never looks at waiters, my dear. It isn't done.

(*He feels he has scored off his wife here and shows secret satisfaction.*)

MAYBELLE. You must go at once and apologise, Pa.

BUTTONS. Don't worry, miss. He's not the Prince.

ALL. Not the Prince ?

BUTTONS. Not he. He's only the valet. Changed places, you know—just for a joke, they say.

BLUEBELLE. Then we haven't spoilt our chances.

(*A sudden dreadful thought convulses the* BARON.)

BARON. I say !

(*They all look at him.*)

I've just realized.

ALL. What ?

BARON (*pointing off* L.). If that chap wasn't the Prince, then the other chap was.

BARONESS. What other chap ?

BARON. The chap who got us through the gates. I gave *him* tuppence.

Herald — my lord + ladies — the Prince would like to take wine with his guests — (guests dance)

(*All express consternation.*)

HERALD (*off up* C. ; *announcing*). Make way for the Prince. Make way for His Royal Highness, Prince Charming.

BUTTONS. Here he comes.

1-Sister

(*He exits* R.)

BARON. Let's hope it's the *right* one this time.

(*The* BARON *and* BARONESS *stand* R., MAYBELLE *and* BLUEBELLE *stand* L. *The* PRINCE *enters up* C.)

PRINCE (*at the top of the steps ; calling*). Dandini—you lazy fellow, where are you ?

(DANDINI *enters* L.)

Are you attending to my guests ? (*He adopts an air of absent-mindedness and boredom, and quizzes the* BARON *and his family through his glass as he comes down the steps to* C.) *Have you met before.*

DANDINI (*moving to* L. *of the* PRINCE). You have met before, I think, sir. You remember—Baron and Baroness Bamboozle. *sir — This is v*

PRINCE (*quizzing them*). Ah yes, to be sure—quite so—we—er—met at the hunt. *nice to meet you both*

BARONESS (*indicating her daughters*). And Bluebelle and Maybelle.

PRINCE (*before turning to them*). Ah—the two hounds—I remember. *their*

DANDINI. *Daughters*, your Highness.

PRINCE (*seeing the sisters*). Oh, ah, yes, of course—the two daughters. (*He quizzes them through his glass.*) Very charming—*very charming*.

(*The sisters curtsey and simper and begin to giggle under his long stare. The* BARONESS *signs to the* BARON.)

BARONESS (*aside to the* BARON). Let us leave them together.

(*They creep* R. *and exit. The* PRINCE *moves down* R. *with* DANDINI.)

PRINCE. Where do we go from here, Dandini ? (*He whispers.*) I am tongue-tied.

(*While they talk, footmen bring on two tables and four chairs, which they place down* R. *and* L. *The sisters seat themselves at the table* L. BUTTONS *enters* R. *with another tray of drinks and hands them round.*) *Herald*

DANDINI. Very awkward, sir. Would you like me to play Prince again ?

PRINCE (*sternly*). Certainly not ! You've had it !

(DANDINI *sighs his disappointment.*)

Tell me—what does one talk about to such people ?

DANDINI. Local gossip, sir. You're always safe if you discuss the neighbours. of the latest fashion.

PRINCE (*shocked*). Scandalous !

DANDINI. Yes, sir—the more the better. Or—you can ask them about their home life. You never know—they may have interesting hobbies.

PRINCE (*with sudden interest*). Such as ?

DANDINI. That is for *you* to find out, sir. The idea is to keep the ball in play—like lawn tennis, you know.

PRINCE. I see. Well—would you like to—start serving ?

DANDINI (*moving to the sisters and raising his glass*). Ladies— your health !

BLUEBELLE (*forgetting her manners in her delight at being noticed*). Cheerioh ! (*She raises her glass.*)

MAYBELLE (*similarly forgetful*). Chin chin ! (*She rises.*)

PRINCE (*in a puzzled aside to* DANDINI). I shall need an interpreter !

DANDINI. You'll soon get used to the language, sir.

(*The* PRINCE *sits at the table* L. *with* BLUEBELLE. DANDINI *escorts* MAYBELLE *to the table* R., *where they sit and whisper closely together.*)

PRINCE. Do you—play games ?

BLUEBELLE. I'll play anything you like, your Highness.

PRINCE. Ah—you are an athlete.

BLUEBELLE. Oh no—there's nothing foreign about me. I was born in—— (*She mentions a local place name.*)

PRINCE. Do you play squash ?

BLUEBELLE (*still out of her depth*). No objections, I'm sure.

PRINCE. It's a very fast game—squash.

BLUEBELLE. I wouldn't mind that.

PRINCE. What is your favourite game ?

BLUEBELLE (*getting the idea*). Sardines !

PRINCE (*wrinkling his nose*). Sardines ? What sort of a game is that ?

BLUEBELLE (*giggling*). Rather like squash, I should *think*. It's played in the dark, you know.

PRINCE. Sounds *very* fishy. What are the rules ?

BLUEBELLE. First of all you have to go away and hide . . .

PRINCE. I should like that part. All my life I have wanted to go away and hide.

BLUEBELLE (*seizing her chance*). Well, of course, if you'd really like—we could . . .

PRINCE (*with a pre-occupied air*). But it's not so easy, if you're a prince, you know. When I want to go into hiding I have to take off my clothes—

(BLUEBELLE *gives him a scared look.*)

(*he goes innocently on, without looking at her*).—and put on the clothes of my valet. Isn't that so, Dandini ?

(DANDINI, *who is in close conversation with* MAYBELLE *at the table* R., *turns to the* PRINCE.)

DANDINI. What did you say, sir ?

PRINCE (*carelessly*). Oh, never mind. How are you getting off —I mean—how are you getting on ?

DANDINI. Very well, sir. Very well indeed. We have been discussing the latest dances.

MAYBELLE. Would you believe it, Bluebelle—he's never heard of the Pally Glide.

PRINCE (*snatching at any chance to relieve his boredom*). Let us perform this glide.

(*They all rise.* MAYBELLE *takes charge.*)

MAYBELLE. In the Pally Glide—you all link arms.

DANDINI (*watching the* PRINCE's *face*). Is that too—pally for you, sir ?

PRINCE (*raising his elbows*). Not at all.

(*They link up and* MAYBELLE *gives them a lesson. They try it with the orchestra. The* BARON *and* BARONESS *enter* R. *and speak through the music.*)

BARONESS. Isn't it charming, Oswald, to see the young couples enjoying themselves ?

BARON (*who has had another drink*). Come along, my dear, let's be young, too.

(They try the dance from their side. Other guests enter and join in. The scene is now working up to the climax of CINDERELLA'S *entry. The* HERALD *enters up* C. *His loud voice stops the action. All face upstage.)*

HERALD *(at the top of the steps).* The Princess has arrived!

(In the silence which follows, he repeats his announcement. The PRINCE *steps forward.)*

PRINCE. Princess! What princess?
HERALD. She didn't say, Your Highness.
PRINCE *(puzzled).* Didn't say?
HERALD. She just said—" *The* Princess ", sir.
PRINCE. Where is she?
HERALD *(stepping to one side).* She is here!

*(*CINDERELLA *enters up* C. *and comes slowly down the steps. All eyes are on her. The* PRINCE *bows low.)*

CINDERELLA *(looking around).* Oh—I—I hope I'm not interrupting the proceedings.
PRINCE *(with a significant look at* DANDINI*).* Proceed with the—er—proceedings. *(He takes* CINDERELLA'S *hand and leads her downstage.)* Will the Princess be pleased to accompany me?

(Tabs begin to close as they come down. They pass through and move to the table which has been placed well down R. *The tabs shut off the rest of the scene. They sit at the table.)*

We can talk here, Princess. These are my private quarters. No one can see us here.

(As they are now the only ones who can be seen, this line is intended to get a laugh, and should not be thrown away.)

CINDERELLA *(disappointed).* But I wish to be seen. I wish to make a sensation.
PRINCE *(smiling).* Don't worry—you've made it. Your entrance was superb. Forgive me for asking—but—have you done this sort of thing before?
CINDERELLA. What sort of thing?
PRINCE. Well—it *is* gate-crashing really—isn't it?
CINDERELLA *(innocently).* Your gate was open—nobody stopped me.
PRINCE. How grateful I am for that.

CINDERELLA.   Weren't you expecting me ?

PRINCE.   I was waiting for something to happen—I didn't know what.   You can see how preoccupied I was when you arrived.   I had even been persuaded to take part in some tribal dance.   It was quite beneath me.

CINDERELLA.   It seemed to be beneath everyone else, too. They were all looking down at their feet.

PRINCE.   Until you appeared and then they all looked up.

CINDERELLA.   Including the Prince ?

PRINCE.   Including the Prince.   And now the Prince feels that he doesn't want to see any of them again—ever.   In fact, he's thinking of sending them all away.

CINDERELLA.   He mustn't do that.   I want to dance.

PRINCE.   We can dance—just you and I.

CINDERELLA.   But I want to feel that a thousand eyes are on me.

PRINCE.   A thousand !   (*He gives a little whistle of surprise.*)   I can't run to that—not even for a princess.

CINDERELLA.   *The* Princess !

PRINCE.   I beg your pardon—*The* Princess !

CINDERELLA (*naively*).   I don't know whether you have noticed, but my dress is something quite exceptional.   (*She rises and turns around to exhibit it.*)

PRINCE (*rising and quizzing through his glass*).   It is indeed. What do they call it—in the trade ?   A creation ?

CINDERELLA (*with a far-away look*).   It *has* been created—for me—out of nothing.

PRINCE.   That's a secret the trade would like to know.

CINDERELLA.   *I* changed, too, when I put it on.

PRINCE.   Of course you did.

CINDERELLA.   I mean—I became a different person.   It is all very strange.   I don't even remember my past.

PRINCE (*with a smile*).   So much the better.   No one wants a woman with a past.

CINDERELLA.   I seem to have forgotten everything—except how to dance and sing.

PRINCE.   Princess, will you dance for me—here ?

CINDERELLA.   But there is no room.

PRINCE.   Then—will you sing for me ?

CINDERELLA.   On one condition.

PRINCE.   What is that ?

CINDERELLA.   You are to take me back among your guests and dance with me.

PRINCE. That's a bargain. Wait—an idea has come to me. You shall have your thousand eyes, Princess. We will have a spot dance and I will arrange for the spot-light to rest on you—always.

CINDERELLA (*laughing*). Is that quite *fair*?

PRINCE. All's fair—in love!

(*A song number here for the* PRINCESS *or a duet, if desired, which takes them off. The tabs re-open. The dancing in the ballroom has been abandoned. Only the* BARON'S *family remain and they are speaking their minds as usual.*)

BARONESS. If you ask *me*—I should say that the whole thing has been *arranged*.

BARON. Devilish fine girl, anyway.

BARONESS (*swooping on him*). How do *you* know?

BARON (*hastily*). I was alluding to her *tout ensemble*.

BARONESS (*sharply*). What is that?

BARON. French, my dear.

BARONESS (*suspiciously*). Is it improper?

BARON. Not at all.

BARONESS. Then why say it in *French*?

(*The* BARON *throws up his hands despairingly and turns away.*)

BARONESS. I've seen her face before, though I can't think where.

BLUEBELLE. And *I've* seen her dress before, somewhere.

MAYBELLE. In the window?

BLUEBELLE. That's right. It was in the sale at (*she mentions the name of a local draper*).

MAYBELLE. And did you notice the way she *moved*? Bow-legged, I should say!

(DANDINI *enters* R.)

DANDINI. I hope, Baron, that you and your charming family are enjoying yourselves.

BARON (*with sarcasm*). We're having a perfectly delightful evening. Everything in the garden is lovely.

DANDINI (*taking him literally*). So you've been round the garden?

BARON. Well—not—er—geographically. It was just a *façon de parler*.

DANDINI. What is that?

BARON. French, sir.

BARONESS.   Oswald—are you at it again?

BARON.   I was just telling our young friend what a gorgeous time we're having.

BARONESS (*meaningly*).   I hope *other people* (*she glances off*) are having a gorgeous time, too.

BLUEBELLE.   Do you think the Prince is having a gorgeous time?

DANDINI.   Extremely probable, madam. (*He looks off.*) His Highness is—very susceptible.

BARONESS.   Young man, you can't hoodwink *me* with those long words.

MAYBELLE.   Is she an actress?

DANDINI.   I don't know.

BARONESS.   She is *not* on the stage. (*She looks around the stage significantly.*) That's what the hold-up's about.

(*The* HERALD *enters up* C.)

HERALD.   My Lords and Ladies—the next dance, by special request, will be a Spot Dance. Please take your partners.

(*He exits up* C. *Waltz music begins. The* GUESTS *enter* R. *and* L. *The lights are dimmed except for a spotlight on the steps up* C. *The* PRINCE *and* CINDERELLA *enter up* C., *come down the steps and start dancing together. The* GUESTS *join in. The* BARONESS *dances with the* BARON. MAYBELLE *and* BLUEBELLE *dance together. The spotlight moves over the dancers and picks up the* BARON's *family now and again and they struggle to keep in the beam, but when the music suddenly stops, the light is on the* PRINCE *and* CINDERELLA, *who are* C. *The* HERALD *enters up* C. *He carries a bouquet.*)

BARONESS (*in a loud aside to the* BARON).   I *said* it had been *arranged*.

(*The* HERALD *presents the bouquet to* CINDERELLA, *then retires up* C. *The* GUESTS *applaud. The* PRINCE *and* CINDERELLA *bow their acknowledgments. The music and dance are resumed. The* PRINCE *and* CINDERELLA *dance up* R. *and are lost to view. Twelve o'clock begins to strike. The loud chimes are clearly heard through the music. Unseen by the audience,* CINDERELLA *exits up* R.)

PRINCE (*shouting suddenly*).   Stop the music!

(*The beam of the spotlight picks him out. All music and movement stops suddenly. The last strokes of midnight are heard.*)

D

(*He moves* C.) Bring up the lights!

(*As the lights come up, the* PRINCE *gazes distractedly around.*
DANDINI *runs to him.*)

DANDINI. What has happened, sir?
PRINCE (*ignoring the question*). Did you see her go?
DANDINI. Who, sir?
PRINCE. The Princess, you fool!
DANDINI. The Princess! Gone?
PRINCE. Vanished—out of my very arms. Look for her—she
mustn't go like that.

(DANDINI *exits hurriedly up* C. *The* PRINCE *runs off down* R.
Their places C. *are taken by the* BARON *and his family.*)

BARONESS (*breaking the silence*). Another pre-arrangement, I
shouldn't wonder.
BARON. I don't think so. The Prince seemed to be genuinely
upset.
BLUEBELLE. She must be mental.
MAYBELLE. Crackers!
BARONESS. She's nothing of the kind. I tell you it's all a
put-up job.
BARON. How can he put her up if she's gone?
BARONESS (*aside to* BARON). They're going to *elope*. I know
the signs. (*She turns to her daughters.*) Bluebelle! Maybelle!
Follow me! This is no place for innocent young girls.
BARON (*disappointed*). Are you going to call it a day, already?
BARONESS. I won't say here what I'm going to call it. In any
case *we're* going home.

(*She hustles her protesting daughters off* L. *The* BARON *follows
reluctantly.* DANDINI *enters up* C. *He carries the slipper. The*
PRINCE *re-enters down* R. *His face falls as he sees* DANDINI'S
expression.)

PRINCE. Don't tell me. I can see by your face you haven't
found her.
DANDINI. She must have been in a great hurry, sir. She left
one of her slippers behind. It was picked up by one of your
sentries.
PRINCE (*crestfallen*). That means she's got away.

(DANDINI *comes down the steps to* C. *Start incidental music here, leading up to a slow curtain. The music from the song recently sung by the* PRINCE *and* CINDERELLA *can be used, if suitable.*)

One of her slippers. (*The* PRINCE *faces front and speaks mechanically, as if in a dream.*) So that is all that is left of my dream of happiness—one of her slippers!

(*There is a pause as he gazes with a sad expression at the slipper which* DANDINI *holds out. The* GUESTS *all look sympathetic.*)

Life is hard, Dandini.

DANDINI (*gently*).   Do you wish to take it, sir?

PRINCE (*hopelessly*).   My life?

DANDINI (*embarrassed*).   The *slipper*, sir.

PRINCE (*still dreamy and vague*).   Take the slipper . . . ?

DANDINI.   It might—come in useful, sir—as a keepsake.

PRINCE (*taking the slipper with great care*).   A keepsake—from the only girl I ever loved!

He turns with a dejected air and walks slowly to the steps up C. *The* GUESTS *withdraw to* R. *and* L. *as he goes between them. The* CURTAIN *slowly falls, to rise again immediately on a picture of the* PRINCE *on the steps, where he holds up the slipper and gazes fondly at it. The* GUESTS *dress the stage in sympathetic attitudes.* DANDINI, *with drooping head and folded arms, stands* L.C. *The music reaches a climax as—*

                    the CURTAIN *falls.*

SCENE 6

SCENE.—*Outside the castle.*

Before the CURTAIN *rises, heavy and prolonged snoring is heard.*

When the CURTAIN *rises, it is night, and* SPY *is seen in the moonlight leaning against the closed gates, fast asleep. After a few moments,* COP *enters* R., *moves to* SPY *and shakes him.*

COP.   Hi! Wake up!

            (SPY *wakes up slowly and looks sleepily at* COP.)

SPY (*thickly*).   Halt—who goes there?

Cop. It's a bit late to say that, isn't it? I've been hanging over you for some time. I could have shot you more than once.

Spy. Once is enough. Don't waste your ammo.

Cop. Now listen. I've found out where that bit o' stuff went.

Spy. What bit o' stuff?

Cop. You know—that girl who was running away and dropped her shoe. I chased her. She ran full tilt into Baron Bamboozle's house. Now—here's a queer thing. When she ran into that house she hadn't got her fine dress on.

Spy (*looking interested for the first time*). She hadn't got it on?

Cop. I swear she hadn't.

Spy (*rising*). Are you prepared to swear to what she had got on?

Cop. She was wearing a dirty old dress as far as *I* could see.

Spy. Same girl?

Cop. Same girl.

(Spy *gives* Cop *a sly look.*)

Spy. You didn't see any elephants wearing pink trunks, did you?

Cop. Now look 'ere, Spy—I haven't had anything to drink, and you know it.

Spy. Then—what happened to the fine dress?

Cop. Search me!

Spy. Ah, now we're getting somewhere. (*He begins to search* Cop's *clothing.*)

Cop. Here—stop that! When I say, "search me", I don't mean search *me*. I mean—search my mind, see?

Spy. Where d'you keep that?

Cop. If I hadn't had brains, what d'you think would have happened to you—years ago? D'you know I could get you court-martialled for this?

Spy. For what?

Cop. Sleepin' on yer post.

Spy. I wasn't! I was sleeping down there. (*He points to the ground by the gates.*)

Cop. What did you do with that shoe?

Spy. Took it up to the castle. Gave it to a chap who came out as if he'd lost something, too. He said the Prince was looking for the owner. He said there'd probably be a reward——Blimey! (*The situation begins to dawn on him.*) We're the men! We've got the gen.

Cop. Sh! Someone's coming!

(*They creep* R. *and exit. The* PRINCE *enters through the gates.*)

PRINCE (*in soliloquy*).   A lovely night—and no one to share it.

(*The* FAIRY GODMOTHER *enters* L.)

GODMOTHER.   Cheer up, young sir. Don't look so woe-begone.

PRINCE.   And who may *you* be?

GODMOTHER (*artfully*).   If I were to tell you—you wouldn't believe me.

PRINCE.   What is your business?

GODMOTHER.   Marriage.

PRINCE (*with a mirthless laugh*).   You flatter yourself.

GODMOTHER.   Not my marriage. And yet your marriage. Can you solve that one? (*She chuckles.*)

PRINCE.   Upon my soul, you are a strange old party, and no mistake. (*He looks hard at her and turns away.*) There is a queer light in your eye.

GODMOTHER.   It's an eye that sees a lot. Things are not going well with you, are they?

PRINCE.   Alas!

GODMOTHER.   The course of true love never did run smooth.

PRINCE.   My true love has vanished.

GODMOTHER.   Don't stand there, then—twiddling your thumbs. The girl you stand and wait for never comes.

PRINCE.   You speak in rhyme. Can you tell fortunes, too?

GODMOTHER.   Sometimes.

PRINCE.   I will pay you well.

GODMOTHER.   I don't want your money. Give me your hand.

PRINCE (*laughing*).   My hand—in marriage?

GODMOTHER (*sternly*).   Your hand—in good faith.

PRINCE.   Here it is. (*He holds out his hand.*)

(*The* FAIRY GODMOTHER *peers into his palm.*)

The light is too dim. You cannot see.

GODMOTHER.   I have seen all I need to see. You want your Princess back?

PRINCE.   With all my heart.

GODMOTHER.   To marry her?

PRINCE (*fervently*).   Without delay!

GODMOTHER (*looking again into his palm*).   A marriage has been arranged and will shortly take place . . .

PRINCE (*withdrawing his hand with an impatient gesture*).   But I have lost my bride.

GODMOTHER. Find her.

PRINCE. How?

GODMOTHER (*business-like; turning to go*). Make inquiries. Try asking the first person you meet. That will do for a start.

(*The* PRINCE *turns to question her again, but she has disappeared* L.)

PRINCE. What a strange old party. Does she really know something? I wonder! " Try asking the first person you meet ", she said.

(SPY *enters* R.)

The sentry! Why—of course—the sentry. Hi! Sentry!

Excuse me can you help me — have

(SPY *moves to the* PRINCE.)

When you were on your beat, did you see a lady in a hurry?

SPY (*thinking slowly*) Let me think. In a hurry, you say? Was she in a party frock as well?

PRINCE (*eagerly*). Yes.

SPY. Fair hair?

PRINCE. Yes, yes!

SPY. Blue eyes?

PRINCE. Yes, yes, yes!

SPY. Running like a race-horse?

PRINCE (*bursting with excitement*). You saw her?

SPY (*shaking his head*). No.

(*The* PRINCE *turns away in despair.*)

But I know who did.

PRINCE (*turning eagerly again*). Who?

SPY. My mate. (*He jerks his head* R.)

PRINCE. Go and ask him at once.

SPY (*with exasperating slowness*). Well, I'll try, sir—but . . .

PRINCE. What's the matter?

SPY. You see, sir—he's rather a touchy chap, my mate. He doesn't like being asked questions, you know. Specially when he's having his lunch. (*He tries to kill time while he thinks out a plan.*)

PRINCE. But he can't be having his *lunch* at *this* time of the morning.

SPY. He *might* be, sir—you never know. He's an irregular sort of chap—gets a bit dangerous, too, sometimes, and I don't want to get a punch on the nose.

PRINCE. Here—take my purse. You can have what's in it.
(*He gives his purse to* SPY.)

(SPY *looks inside the purse.*)

How d'you feel about it now?

SPY. I feel a bit better, sir.

PRINCE. Good! Now, look here. I've got a lady's slipper
and I'm going to find the owner if I have to go down on my
bended knees to the lowest in the land.

SPY (*in his best butler's manner*). I wouldn't do anything like
that, sir, if I were you, sir—if you'll excuse my mentioning it.
For a man of your standing, sir, there are other ways and means—
if you won't mind my saying so.

PRINCE (*equally polite*). Not at all—I want all the help I can get.

(SPY *pulls out a note-book and pencil.*)

SPY. Might I suggest, sir, an advertisement . . .

PRINCE (*snatching the book and pencil*). That's a fine idea!
We'll advertise in the—— (*He mentions a local paper.*) Now,
let me see—what shall we write—" Lost or strayed "—no, that's
for cats and dogs, isn't it?

SPY. Excuse me, sir. (*He politely but firmly takes back the
book and pencil.*) Will you allow me to draw up the announcement for you? I have had much experience in these matters.
I—er—I used to work for British Railways.

PRINCE (*showing great surprise*). British Railways?

SPY. Yes, sir. In the lost property office, sir!

PRINCE. You're a smart chap. You ought to get promotion.

SPY. Would you be prepared, sir, to offer me promotion if I
find the girl?

(*The* PRINCE *gives him a sharp look.*)

The—er—the young lady, I beg your pardon, sir.

PRINCE. If you do that, I'll recommend you for sergeant.

SPY (*driving a hard bargain*). Could you make it Sergeant-
Major, sir? It's a risky job.

PRINCE (*turning to go*). All right—Sergeant-Major. (*He moves
L. and turns.*) Carry on, Sergeant-Major!

SPY (*grinning at his thoughts*). I won't half give that sergeant a
walloping. (*He hits his palm with the note-book several times.*)

(COP *enters* R.)

It's all right, Cop, my boy—I've fixed it.

COP (*aggressively*).   *You've* fixed it!

SPY.   Yes. And I'm for promotion.

COP (*with growing resentment*).   *You're* for promotion!

SPY.   Yes. Sergeant-Major.

COP.   And what do *I* get?

SPY (*re-assuring him*).   Oh, you'll get a stripe, I expect.

COP (*moving to him*).   I'll get a stripe, will I? Let me get this straight. I'm to get a stripe and you're to get a crown?

SPY.   That's right.

COP.   For sleepin' on yer post!

SPY (*looking round anxiously*).   Sh!

COP (*turning to the audience*).   Well—of all the . . .

SPY *claps a hand quickly over* COP'S *mouth as the lights black-out and—*

the CURTAIN *falls.*

SCENE 8

SCENE.—*The throne-room.*

> *The back of the stage is raised, and wide steps up* C, *lead from it. There are entrances* R. *and* L. *The throne stands at an angle up* R.

When the CURTAIN *rises,* BUTTONS *is seated on the throne and the* CHORUS, *as Ladies of the Court, are grouped around him. He wears improvized robes and a cheap crown which has been knocked sideways by preceding horse-play. All laugh merrily.*

BUTTONS (*rising with mock dignity*).   *Ladies!*

> (*The* CHORUS *stop laughing.*)

If there is any more unseemly behaviour, I shall dismiss the Court.

> (*There is a renewed burst of laughter from the* CHORUS.)

That's done it! You're dismissed. Out you go—all of you. (*He chases the* CHORUS *off* R. *and* L., *eventually getting entangled in his robes and collapsing* C.) I can't get anyone to take me seriously.

(BUTTONS *has the stage now and there is an opportunity for him to sing an appropriate song, supported by the* CHORUS, *if desired. After the number, the stage is left empty. Then the* HERALD *enters up* R., *followed by two* FOOTMEN, *who carry, in stately fashion, the chair for the ceremony. After much experimenting, the chair is placed to the* HERALD'S *satisfaction* R.C. BUTTONS *re-enters, in his uniform, bearing a footstool which he places in front of the chair. The* FOOTMEN *retire up stage, taking positions on each side of the steps up* C. BUTTONS *and* HERALD *are still fussing about with the chair and footstool when* DANDINI *enters down* L.)

DANDINI.   What's the big idea?

HERALD.   We are carrying out the Prince's special orders.

BUTTONS (*importantly*).   There's going to be an operation.

DANDINI.   An operation? In the throne-room?

BUTTONS.   The Prince said so. "Operation Shoehorn", he said it was.

HERALD.   Some of the ladies are here, already waiting. They say there's been an advertisement.

DANDINI (*laughing*).   What for? A foot-clinic?

HERALD.   They don't seem to know. They are all very high ladies, sir.

DANDINI.   How high?

HERALD (*producing four visiting cards and reading*).   " The Duchess of Gorgonzola, Lady Camembert, Madame Stilton and the Countess Cheddar."

DANDINI.   Sounds like a deputation from the Food Office.

HERALD.   They were all at the ball the other evening.

DANDINI.   Really? I didn't smell—I mean I didn't see them.

HERALD.   Shall I show them in, sir?

DANDINI.   I suppose so.

(*The* HERALD *exits up* C.)

and
Buttons, go and tell His Highness that some very high ladies have arrived.

(BUTTONS *moves to the exit up* L.)

and
He calls.) ~~Oh, Buttons~~—you'd better open the windows on your way out.

BUTTONS *exits up* L. *The* HERALD *enters up* C., *and stands at the top of the steps.* DANDINI *stands* R.C.)

Not necessary

HERALD (*announcing*). The Duchess of Gorgonzola.

(*The* DUCHESS *enters up* C. *and comes down the steps.*)

DUCHESS (*to* DANDINI; *with animation*). I've come in answer to the advertisement.

DANDINI. Oh, yes. (*He points down* L.) Would your Grace be so good as to stand over there.

DUCHESS. Stand? (*She points to the chair* R.C.) Can't I sit there?

DANDINI. I regret—it is reserved.

DUCHESS. For whom?

DANDINI. For the—er—operation.

DUCHESS. Operation? How thrilling! (*She moves down* L.)

HERALD (*announcing*). Lady Camembert and Madame Stilton.

(LADY CAMEMBERT *and* MADAME STILTON *enter up* C. *and come down the steps.*)

LADY CAMEMBERT. We're *so* excited. Is there *really* a reward and have we *all* got a chance?

MADAME STILTON (*drawling*). What's it all in aid of?

DANDINI (*pointing down* L.). Will the ladies be pleased to stand over there?

LADY CAMEMBERT. No seats? How quaint!

MADAME STILTON (*crossly*). Like a snack-bar!

(*They move down* L.)

HERALD (*announcing*). The Countess Cheddar.

(*The* COUNTESS CHEDDAR *enters up* C. *and comes down the steps. As she does so, the* PRINCE *enters up* L., *and overhears the* COUNTESS'S *speech. He carries the slipper and a scroll.*)

COUNTESS (*to* DANDINI). I hope we're not being made fools of, young man. I've got a feeling it's all a try-on.

(DANDINI *waves the* COUNTESS *down* L. *The* PRINCE *moves* C. BUTTONS *enters up* L., *and moves to the chair* R.C.)

PRINCE. The Countess is perfectly right. It *is* a try-on. A try-on of this little slipper. (*He places the slipper on the footstool, straightens up, surveys the ladies through his glass with initial eagerness but subsequent disappointment at not seeing what he hoped for, then moves to the throne and sits.*) Are there no more ladies?

HERALD (*looking off*).   Some more just arriving, sir.

(*The* BARONESS, *the* BARON, BLUEBELLE *and* MAYBELLE *enter up* C.
and come down the steps. The sisters move down L.)

PRINCE (*with a low groan*).   That family again!

BARONESS (*to the* HERALD; *with her most winning smile*).   I *hope*
we're not too late.

HERALD.   No, my Lady—the operation is about to take place.

BARONESS.   Operation? (*She looks disappointed.*)

HERALD.   A fitting operation, my Lady.

BARONESS.   Will it be painful?

BARON (*who has noticed the slipper*).   Yes, my dear—if *you* have
a fit.

BARONESS (*turning sharply to the* BARON).   I am *not* subject to
fits, Oswald. I am here to support my daughters. You and I
will take a back seat—over there. (*She points down* R).

BARON.   But that's the way to the *front* seats, my dear.

BARONESS.   Don't argue, Oswald. I know what to do. (*She
moves down* R.)

(*The* BARON *starts to follow, but is intercepted by the* HERALD.)

HERALD.   Only *ladies* are eligible, sir.

BARON.   It's all right, Officer. I'm here to support my wife—
(*he nudges the* HERALD) in case she has a fit. (*He chuckles and
moves down* R.)

(*The* HERALD *moves to the* PRINCE, *takes the scroll from him, then
moves* C.)

HERALD (*reading from the scroll*).   " Whereas this delicate piece
of footwear, hereinafter known as the slipper, was left behind at
the Prince's ball, the Lady Claimant, hereinafter known as the
Slipper-fitter—must put her foot in it——"

(*The ladies giggle.*)

(*He glares around.*)   I repeat—" the Lady Claimant, hereinafter
known as the Slitter-fipper—(*he tries again*) hereinafter known as
the Sitter-flipper——"

BARON (*aside to the* BARONESS).   Now he's put *his* foot in it.

(*The* HERALD *becomes confused, but saves himself by deep breathing
and an heroic effort.*)

HERALD (*reading*).   "—hereinafter known as the Slipper-fitter" (*he looks relieved*) " must put her foot in it in the presence of the company here assembled and without benefit of shoe-horn." (*He looks around with an air of triumphant achievement, then resumes reading.*) " In the event of the fitter slipping—in the event of the flipper———" (*He breaks down again.*)

DANDINI (*snatching the scroll from the* HERALD). Here—let *me* read it. (*He reads.*) " Whereas this delicate piece of footwear, hereinafter known as the slipper, was left behind at the Prince's ball, the Lady Claimant, hereinafter known as the Slipper-fitter—" (*He looks at the* HERALD *in a superior way.*) It's quite easy. (*He resumes reading somewhat quicker.*) "—hereinafter known as the Slipper-fitter, must put her foot in it in the presence of the company here assembled, and without benefit of shoe-horn." (*He is now over-confident.*) " In the event of the sitter—flipping —in the event of the flipper . . ."

BUTTONS (*snatching the scroll*). Let *me* read the flipping thing! I'll give it to you in the King's English. It means—Ladies, have a go!

BLUEBELLE. Why didn't he say so? We'll have a go, won't we?

MAYBELLE. I'll have a go, anyway.

LADIES. We'll all have a go.

(*They press forward, the sisters pushing their way to the front. DANDINI intervenes.*)

DANDINI. Now ladies, please! One at a time, one at a time. (*To* BLUEBELLE.) This lady is first. (*He indicates the* DUCHESS.)

MADAME STILTON (*to the sisters*). Get in the queue, yueue!

(*Led by the* DUCHESS, *the four ladies try on the slipper without success. Each lady returns to her position* L. DANDINI *acts as Master of Ceremonies and* BUTTONS, *kneeling at the chair, takes charge of the slipper.* DANDINI *fills in the pauses with remarks such as* " Her foot is too large " " Her instep is too high", *etc., etc. While the fourth lady is in the chair, the Prince interrupts*

PRINCE (*impatiently*). This is a waste of time!

DANDINI. There are still two more to go, sir.

(*He indicates the sisters, who are now jockeying for position.*)

PRINCE (*bored*). Must we go on?

HERALD (*very shocked*). Your Highness advertised in the —— (*He names a local paper.*) What would the editor think if you did not proceed in accordance with the terms of the announcement?

PRINCE. But the editor isn't going to try on the slipper!

HERALD (*woodenly*). It would affect his circulation, sir.

BUTTONS (*holding up the slipper as the last lady vacates the chair*).
Not 'arf it wouldn't!

PRINCE (*to the* HERALD). Go and see if any more ladies have
turned up. (*To* DANDINI.) Carry on.

(*The* HERALD *bows and exits up* C. DANDINI *signs to the sisters,
who make a rush for the chair.* BLUEBELLE *gets there first.*)

BLUEBELLE. I am two years ahead of you.

MAYBELLE. I don't see what *age* has got to do with it.

BLUEBELLE (*holding up her foot with the slipper on it*). Why, it's
gone on easily and it's ever so comfy.

DANDINI (*with frigid emphasis*). Madam has not got the heel in.

BLUEBELLE (*confidently*). Look again, young man.

(DANDINI *examines her foot more closely.*)

DANDINI (*firmly*). No, madam—the heel is *not* in.

(*The* PRINCE *leans forward anxiously.*)

PRINCE. What is it? What is it?

DANDINI. A near-miss, Your Highness.

MAYBELLE. I said you were *passée*—so pass out. (*She jostles*
BLUEBELLE *out of the chair and sits.*)

(BLUEBELLE *goes to the* BARONESS *and makes protesting gestures.*
MAYBELLE *produces a large shoe-horn.*)

DANDINI (*taking the shoe-horn from* MAYBELLE). Madam will
excuse . . .

MAYBELLE (*indignantly*). That's mine!

DANDINI (*politely*). Madam need not worry. It will be
returned to her.

MAYBELLE. But I can't get the slipper on with . . . it—

DANDINI. Madam forgets that the announcement said *distinctly* " without benefit of shoe-horn."

MAYBELLE (*blustering*). It *didn't* say so, distinctly. Nobody
said *anything* distinctly. You couldn't read it *yourself*, so there.
Give it me back, your rude thing. (*She snatches the shoe-horn from*
DANDINI *and joins her family, looking hurt.*)

(*The* HERALD *enters up* C.)

PRINCE. What news?

HERALD. There is another—(*he hesitates*) another *person*, sir.

PRINCE (*puzzled*).   Person?

HERALD (*stiffly*).   I could hardly call her a *lady*, sir.   She appears to be under arrest.

PRINCE.   Under arrest?

HERALD (*contemptuously*).   Under escort, sir.   A kind of Sergeant-Major and a sort of lance-corporal.

(CINDERELLA, *escorted by* SPY *and* COP, *enters up* C.   *She wears her rag-dress.* SPY *wears an exaggerated sergeant-major crown on his arm, and* COP *has a stripe on each arm and a few extra ones on his trouser-legs.*)

PRINCE (*rising quickly and moving to the steps*).   The Princess! *My* Princess.

(CINDERELLA, *very self-possessed, in spite of her dress, smiles sweetly and comes down the steps.*)

SPY (*saluting*).   All present and correct, sir.

(*The* PRINCE *takes* CINDERELLA'S *hand, and they whisper together.*)

BARONESS.   Princess!   What is he talking about?   It's Cinderella.

BARON.   God bless my soul, it's Cinders.

BLUEBELLE.   And out with a couple of soldiers, too.

MAYBELLE (*scolding* BLUEBELLE).   You didn't lock the scullery door.

BARONESS (*pointing to* COP).   Isn't that the man who tried to put my head in a bag?

BARON (*with a chuckle*).   He's had promotion!

PRINCE.   And what is your *real* name, Princess?

CINDERELLA.   Cinderella, Your Highness.

PRINCE (*facing front with a rapt expression*).   Cinderella!   A beautiful name for a beautiful lady.   Make way for Cinderella. Make way for Cinderella.   (*He leads her to the chair, kneels and himself fits on the slipper.*)

(DANDINI *examines the fit.*)

DANDINI.   A perfect fit, Your Highness.

PRINCE.   Cinderella—I had made a vow that I would ask the hand in marriage of the lady whose foot should fit this little slipper. I am here to fulfil that vow.   (*He entreats her.*)

CINDERELLA.   Here is my hand, good Prince—with all my heart.

(*As the* PRINCE *bends over and kisses* CINDRELLA'S *hand, the* BARONESS, *struggling for words, falls back on her old gag.*)

BARONESS.   Didn't I say it had all been arranged?

(*The* FAIRY GODMOTHER *enters up* C.)

GODMOTHER.   But who arranged it? Who arranged it all, I say?

(*She moves down* C. CINDERELLA *rises, and with only one slipper on, runs to the* FAIRY GODMOTHER *and embraces her.*)

CINDERELLA.   My Fairy Godmother!

GODMOTHER.   Now child, don't make a fuss before all these people—and don't run about with only one shoe on—you'll get a ladder.

CINDERELLA.   I haven't *got* the other shoe now.

GODMOTHER (*producing the second slipper; with a chuckle*). Here it is. Put it on child—you don't want to look *odd* in front of your Prince.

(CINDERELLA *puts the slipper on. The* PRINCE *embraces her. The* FAIRY GODMOTHER *watches them with benevolence.*)

GODMOTHER.   So ends the play! Your dream at last come true. I always thought it *would*, though—didn't you?

Cinderella—come now, drop your mask!
To speak the epilogue is now your task.

CINDERELLA (*moving down* C.)

Dear audience, before you go away,
There's just one other thing I want you to say.
Our efforts to amuse pray don't be hard on,
And for our faults accord your gracious pardon.
As Shakespeare wrote—he always put it right,
" Our true intent is all for your delight."

The music for the finale commences. The CHORUS *close in behind the Principals. During the finale, the Principals divide and the* CHORUS *come through them. The Principals exit* R. *and* L., *pass behind and re-enter in pairs up* C. *for the—*

GRAND FINALE.

Prince: lets procede with the
celebration
you are all invited to
the wedding.

PROPERTY LIST

SCENE 1.

Linen bag (SPY)
Linen bag (COP).
Riding-crop (BARON).
Basket. *In it:* prop sandwiches, prop chicken (BUTTONS).
Basket. *In it:* bottle of barley water, glass (BUTTONS).
Bundle of twigs, basket (CINDERELLA).

SCENE 2.

Pram. *In it:* doll with black face, doll with white face, bundle of washing, wig (COP).
Coins (SERGEANT).

SCENE 3.

Table.
Chair.
Stool.
Other furnishings and properties as desired.
Cravat (BARON).
Flower (BUTTONS).
Sedan-chair or other suitable transport for Cinderella.

SCENE 4.

2 rifles (SPY and COP).
Bucket (COP).
Bottle of lemonade (BOY).
Dark glasses, umbrella, ear-trumpet (GRANDPA).
Megaphone (GUIDE).
Old socks (MAN).
Whistle (SERGEANT).
Collecting boxes (SPY and COP).
Purse with coins (PRINCE).

SCENE 5.

2 trays of drinks (BUTTONS).
2 tables.
4 chairs.
Quizzing-glass (PRINCE).
Bouquet (HERALD).

SCENE 6.

Purse (PRINCE).
Note-book and pencil (SPY).

SCENE 7.

Chair (FOOTMEN).
Footstool (BUTTONS).
4 visiting cards (HERALD).
Scroll (PRINCE).
Shoe-horn (MAYBELLE).